ALL TOGETHER NOW
An Alternative View of Theatre and the Community

In this lively and controversial book Steve Gooch, himself a playwright with extensive experience of community theatre, looks at the relationship of present-day theatre to the community in which it takes place. Taking the work of contemporary 'community theatre' as a stimulus, he gives a 'behind-the-scenes' analysis of the failure of commercial theatre – in the subsidised sector as well as the West End – to transcend the mechanisms of box-office and tradition, and to play a vital and integral part in the life of its audience. Examining the initiatives of small theatres and touring companies in the seventies, Gooch looks critically at their work practices and forms of organisation, and draws some positive pointers for the future.

As much about the internal workings of theatre production as about the content and outward face of its shows, *All Together Now* offers new insights into a culture divided between 'high and low', 'popular and serious'.

A METHUEN THEATREFILE

in series with

OTHER SPACES: NEW THEATRE AND THE RSC
by Colin Chambers

THE IMPROVISED PLAY: THE WORK OF MIKE LEIGH
by Paul Clements

THE PLAYS OF EDWARD BOND
by Tony Coult

UNDERSTUDIES: THEATRE AND SEXUAL POLITICS
by Michelene Wandor

PLAYS BY WOMEN: VOLUME ONE
(*Vinegar Tom* by Caryl Churchill; *Dusa, Fish, Stas and Vi* by Pam Gems;
Tissue by Louise Page; *Aurora Leigh* by Michelene Wandor)
Introduced and edited by Michelene Wandor

PLAYS BY WOMEN: VOLUME TWO
(*Rites* by Maureen Duffy; *Letters Home* by Rose Leiman Goldemberg;
Trafford Tanzi by Claire Luckham; *Find Me* by Olwen Wymark)
Introduced and edited by Michelene Wandor

PLAYS BY WOMEN: VOLUME THREE:
(*Aunt Mary* by Pam Gems; *Red Devils* by Debbie Horsfield;
Blood Relations by Sharon Pollock; *Time Pieces* by Lou Wakefield and
The Women's Theatre Group)
Introduced and edited by Michelene Wandor

ALL TOGETHER NOW

An Alternative View
of Theatre and the Community
by

STEVE GOOCH

A Methuen Theatrefile
Methuen · London

For Julia

A METHUEN PAPERBACK
First published as a paperback original in 1984
by Methuen London Ltd, 11 New Fetter Lane, London EC4P 4EE
Copyright © 1984 by Steve Gooch

Typeset by Expression Typesetters
and printed in Great Britain
by Richard Clay (The Chaucer Press) Ltd, Bungay, Suffolk

ISBN 0 413 53480 4

CONTENTS

INTRODUCTION

The idea of theatre relating to, and being a part of, the community from which it originates is neither new nor strange. From the dances and ceremonies of 'primitive' societies through the Greeks and Shakespeare to more recent traditions in British theatre, audiences and the social context in which plays are produced have always been recognised as a significant, if at times obscure, element of theatre history. In a medium where the immediate presence of its public is so crucial, this is no surprise. The surprise is that 'community theatre', a term which implies the attempt to bring artefact and public closer together, should be viewed as something special.

One may remain sceptical about exactly *how* broad the audiences were in Shakespeare's London, Calderon's Madrid, or for Victorian spectacle, but there is no doubt that theatre, since the arrival of television, has become increasingly the specialised preserve of a minority of enthusiasts. Yet while such minority art forms continue to enjoy the detailed respect of the universities, publishing houses, 'quality' newspaper reviewers and their readerships, mass cultural forms like TV, popular music and fashion, which dominate the market-place, are rarely commented on seriously, and then only in general terms or 'sociologese'.

Not only do we have a culture divided into 'high' and 'low', 'serious' and 'popular', 'art' and 'craft', etc., but a culture divided from its public by the market mechanisms of box-office, advertising, publicity and the reviewing industry in such a way that even comment and criticism *about* the arts operate within and reflect the same divisions. Exactly how these divisions arose is a subject to which I hope theatre historians will turn their attention in the near future. What follows in this book, however, is an attempt to report on the effects of those divisions as they operate in the theatre of the present day, how they were encountered by the post-war generation as it entered the theatre in the sixties and seventies, and some pointers to how these divisions may be overcome in the future.

This is not, however, simply a matter of describing the work of theatre companies, or indeed of discussing in the abstract the ideas behind their work (both of which have been attempted in the past), but of examining the relationship of both product *and* content to the methods by which theatre is produced and to how it is received by audiences, practitioners and critics. It is neither history nor literary criticism but an attempt to relate the practice and theory of theatre in our community to the processes of its production and consumption. This requires not only an analysis of the structures of command in theatre production but also some insight into the ways in which individual theatre workers develop both their artistic and imaginative faculties as well as a critical consciousness of the function of their work.

For the generation which grew up in post-war, welfare state Britain, and started work in the theatre after the late sixties, experience of the contradictions in our divided culture was direct and head-on. Since the war, children from all social classes have been equally able (though not equally easily) to move through a formal education system dominated by the liberal and humanitarian values of the minority culture. They have been encouraged to appreciate and examine rigorously the nature of our democracy. At the same time they have witnessed the burgeoning of a brassy and commercial mass culture. While the autonomous power of headmasters and university principals has at times suggested the limits of democracy within the minority culture (during the sit-ins of the late sixties for example), mass culture has at times appeared to offer a kind of liberation – if only from parents and teachers. But the moment one applies those humanitarian educational values to the commercial world of TV, fashion and the 'musibiz', or applies the 'popular' values of mass culture to the Eng. Lit. enclaves of the cultural Establishment, a great many awkward questions arise.

The answer for many people entering cultural life in the seventies and discovering the power of the Civil Service or large business consortia behind TV, or the concentrated power of a few local dignitaries on the boards of theatres supported by public money, was to take all those begged questions on board. A more broadly popular yet socially relevant culture was required, which also needed to be more democratically run.

What follows therefore begins with our inherited culture, goes 'behind the scenes' to examine the process of production in established and then 'fringe' theatre, concluding with the new cultural initiatives suggested by the last fifteen years. Beginning with a run-down of the theatre companies covered by the scope of this book, I have attempted to describe the background of theatre tradition against which they reacted; the aesthetic laws of the medium of theatre itself through which that struggle was conducted; the modification of those laws in the dominant, commercial sector of theatre; the failure of partial subsidy to alter the situation radically; the beginnings of the 'fringe' in opposition to both the content and methods of established theatre; the difficulties of working to new audiences and of co-operative forms of organisation; the problems of constantly generating new material, particularly in the face of recession; then some possibilities of a new approach to the organisation and administration of theatre both nationally and within companies themselves; and finally, coming full circle, the beginnings of the new cultural and aesthetic traditions offered by the movement towards a more community-conscious theatre.

Within this context the term 'community theatre' itself has been subject to considerable abuse. Its syllables were once pronounced individually and aloud to me by a member of a London theatre's board to infer their similarity with 'com-mun-ism'. Sometimes it's assumed that anything so close to home cannot be professional – a misunderstanding experienced and struggled against by many theatre companies (though in America it actually *means* 'amateur' theatre). Sometimes its experimental quality is used as an apology for sloppy thinking or poor production standards. Occasionally its name is taken in vain to extract more subsidy from local authorities. The very totality of its ideological opposition to established theatre – whether in regard to audience, work methods, organisation or product – makes it an unfamiliar and controversial concept. Though levels of subsidy have kept its initiatives small-scale, its achievements are already considerable, and its decade of lessons offers a firm basis for future development.

1: COMMUNITY THEATRE & THEATRE IN THE COMMUNITY

As understood today, the term 'community theatre' is most commonly associated with companies like the Combination at the Albany in Deptford or the Half Moon in East London, whose theatres are based in a particular locality and who see as an important part of their work the generation of a geographically local culture: productions about South or East London; productions by South or East Londoners; productions which South or East Londoners will want to see; productions which in some way express the viewpoint and culture of people in their area. The acting companies are small, working conditions are poor, resources are minimal, audiences rarely large, and the actual relationship with the local community can be fraught with difficulties.

But there are also touring companies, of similar size and working under similar conditions, which do not have a base in which to perform: Solent People's Theatre in Southampton, Pit Prop and North West Spanner in Lancashire, Bruvvers in the North-East, Avon in the South-West, Perspectives in Mansfield, and others. Although not fixed in a particular auditorium these companies, too, see a large part of their job as expressing the interests and concerns of people in their area. Often these areas are urban, and the companies seek to play to predominantly working-class audiences, but there are also community companies in rural areas – Orchard Theatre, Medium Fair, EMMA – where the composition of audience is different in social class, not simply because there are fewer industrial working-class people in these areas, but because the whole structure of community life is different. There are even companies like Welfare State, Red Ladder, Open Cast and TOOT – all quite different from each other – who are able to serve both industrial and rural communities within and beyond their immediate area.

Nevertheless, this identification with a local community doesn't describe the whole intent of these companies' work. The Half Moon, over its ten-year history, has reflected as much European, and more recently American, culture as any home-grown product. The other companies also present classics from time to time, or plays of broader interest. Indeed, if one looks closely at the actual work of the touring companies based in particular regions, one realises that some aspects of it aren't all that dissimilar from the work of the theatre-in-education companies, who see their brief as servicing school-age children within their catchment area. Similarly, much of the product presented under the banner of community theatre is not dissimilar to that of companies like 7:84, Belt and Braces, Broadside Mobile Workers Theatre and CAST, who tour nationally, profess no particular geographic base and yet place a particular emphasis on playing to working-class audiences.

Since the mid-seventies companies like the Women's Theatre Group, Monstrous Regiment, Bloomers, Spare Tyre and many others have identified their work with the women's movement and might be considered to relate to the feminist 'community', while the Black Theatre Co-operative, Tara Arts and Temba have identified with Black, Asian and other minority communities. Other 'alternative theatre' companies have come to be associated with the young adult circuit of student unions, 'fringe' and studio theatres and pubs, whose audiences are reached by the circulation of *Time Out* and *City Limits*. Others ignore their audience in arriving at a definition of their work. They simply do 'new plays of contemporary relevance' or 'shows with a strong musical content'. In these cases we are talking about a community not defined by place or geography but by a constituency of interest, be it a class interest, common social or political concerns, or shared cultural preference.

While not all the companies mentioned above would actually define their work as 'community theatre', some of those who do are more similar to non-community companies than to each other. For example, the Scottish 7:84 Theatre Company, to judge from its name alone, might be seen as specifically addressing 'the Scottish community'; but English 7:84 doesn't view itself self-consciously as servicing 'the English Community' – just as in sport non-English athletes are often referred to as 'the Welshman, 'the Scot' or 'the Irishman' while their English counterparts are called by name. If we were to pursue this idea of definition by locality further, Hampstead Theatre Club, which reflects the interests of an extremely homogenous group within its catchment area, might qualify as the most perfectly realised community theatre in the country! The Theatre Royal at Stratford, East London, the Victoria Theatre at Stoke-on-Trent and the Liverpool Everyman are also very conscious of their local audiences, but their product is hardly community theatre in the recognised, post-seventies sense. Even the National Theatre, whose claims for its catchment area are more grandiose than anyone's – 'The National Theatre is *Your* Theatre' – might see itself qualifying by such a definition.

Geography, preferred audience, the content and style of companies' work and their political consciousness all identify the *trappings* of the community theatre movement; but they don't add up to an explanation of why it exists and why its influence is so far-reaching. While many of these companies have been founded in opposition or as a complement to the limited range of conventional, established theatre – from the West End and national subsidised houses to the regional repertory companies – it is also true that there are as many different rationales, aesthetic approaches, structures of internal organisation and work methods amongst them as there are companies themselves. One might even say there are as many different visions of an alternative theatre as there are individual theatre workers in these companies.

But those same theatre workers might well strenuously deny any tendency towards individualism. They would emphasise the value of the collective approach to their work and point to their intention of reaching a socially broader audience. The concrete examples of this are everywhere, but they are scattered and isolated. The histories of the Association of Community Theatres (TACT) and the Independent Theatre Council (ITC), bodies set up to represent and lobby for the interests of these companies collectively, have achieved nothing like the success or prominence of their counterparts in countries like Sweden and Holland. Magazines like the *SCYPT* (Standing Conference of Young Peoples Theatres) *Journal*, *Platform* and *Performance*, which have responded to the once strident call for an organ to focus attention on this area of work, have received scant support or recognition.

Much of the failure of TACT and ITC must be attributable to the huge variation in aims, forms of organisation and aesthetic approach between the companies involved. Aims and audiences I have already touched on. Organisationally, these companies range from a single individual with a grant who then employs everybody else, to co-operatives where everyone is supposed to participate in every aspect of production – from deciding on the script and arranging the bookings to painting the set. Some companies rehearse conventionally with a director and a script written by one person, while others do without either director or script. There are many gradations between the extremes, the only constant being that a more 'democratic' process generally prevails than in the established theatre.

Given this multiplicity of companies, methods and viewpoints, any assertion about what actually constitutes community theatre is bound to be open to contradiction Indeed, any assertion about theatre in general might well suffer the same fate. For not only have these companies taken the begged social and political questions on board, they have also taken on the aesthetic problems. Throughout the fifties and sixties a succession of foreign theatre companies visited Britain, each offering their own alternative model to our indigenous traditions: first the visits of the Berliner Ensemble from 1956 onwards, then Peter Daubeny's world theatre seasons, then the visits of the Living Theatre, La Mama and other American companies in the mid-sixties. For the generation growing up and watching theatre in this period, the idea of theatre as generally perceived in our society was exploded.

The popular and literary traditions

Since it is as consumers of culture that we first develop any innate inclination we possess for producing it, the visits of foreign theatre companies were obviously critical in shaping that generation's creative objectives. But they took place against the background of a general theatre tradition with its own received history and accepted method of production. That tradition, relying with typically English pragmatism on a number of tested strengths, has proved extremely durable. It is a curious product of folk memory, literary respectability and economic necessity. Its apogee, the drawing-room comedy, is significant not for its intrinsic merit but for what it tells us about that tradition.

It is after all important when examining any tradition in theatre to remember that it is primarily a medium of live performance. Only when a play is performed can it be said to be *produced* (a significant double meaning) – to have taken on a public existence. Consequently only theatre within living memory can be spoken of with any certainty as to the precise qualities it possessed, the thoughts it provoked, the emotions it aroused. Even then, personal prejudice, fond nostalgia, collective mythology and sheer self-deception can transform the memory of what was experienced. Moreover, the quality of communication between the person remembering or recording the event and the person to whom the memory or record is passed on also conditions how it is assessed. Certainly one rarely gains a satisfactory impression of how plays actually are from either reviews or even friends' reports. In the end you have to see the play yourself. In this respect the script itself, the actual written text, though only a partial reflection of actual performance, remains the most 'objective' indication of how the performance actually was.

This has allowed speculation by academics about the exact nature of classical theatre performance, based on a cavalier mixture of textual analysis and the little we know about actual conditions of production, to establish a groundless mythology of what is 'popular' and 'realistic' in our theatre tradition. It is touching that the fusty imagination of academia should be stirred by such speculation, but it is dangerous to allow its amateurish mythologies, rooted in a kind of romantic voyeurism, to become enshrined in popular consciousness: especially when so little hard evidence about performance conditions exists, and when the actual effect of any theatre performance depends so much on the subjective response of the individual. Nevertheless, Green Rooms and rehearsal rooms up and down the country continue to echo with these traditional notions of 'realism' and 'popularity', fuelled by these speculations and subsequently applied to texts written several centuries after Shakespeare.

Anyone with a first-hand knowledge of work in the theatre, if honest, cannot help but assume (though with equally little evidence) that half of Shakespeare's texts were cut in performance and only restored later by a zealous editor or the playwright himself. Even allowing for the added difficulty of today's audiences in understanding Elizabethan English, it's unlikely that what is boring to a popular audience today could have been less boring to an even less sophisticated 'mass' audience then. For a commercial theatre in competition with rival companies where the slightest longueur no doubt meant that the punters would shift their loyalty down the road, such considerations must seriously have qualified what went on stage, how it went, and what the audience got from it.

Alongside the greater speculative freedom which academic and intellectual prejudice can enjoy by ignoring awkward questions about conditions of production and by examining theatre primarily through text only, our present-day system of production in theatre, TV and film has also tended to look on scripts as products in their own right, sometimes even as a commodity (as in the film industry where they're even – perhaps more honestly – called 'properties'). This joint interest of the business and academic worlds in theatre as a product divorced from the quality of its actual communication with its audience has in turn influenced theatre writing itself, which can easily become 'literary' and narrow in its public relevance. At the same time the consideration of plays separately from their production process has tended to distance the less literate sections of society from an interest in theatre. In an age where film and television offer greater accessibility, this separation is thrown into sharper perspective. A double standard has come to operate in our thinking about theatre by which the great classical texts and their intrinsic values are idolised, while in the practical business of production for performance cut-throat, commercial values still apply.

In spite of our tradition being dominated by the 'literary', published texts of the classics, we know that there were travelling players in the late Middle Ages who in some way were connected with the beginnings of religious non-conformism. We also know that the theatre companies of Shakespeare's time were originally travelling companies which took the opportunity to settle in London. There are occasional parallels with our contemporary touring companies here, but there is a sense in which theatre at any point in history is no more than the product of people coming together at a particular time to express what is 'in the air' by simply acting it out, perhaps because no other means of expression is open to them. However, if these people then come to look for continuity and stability in their work, they need premises and a patron – be it a wealthy nobleman, the paying public or the State.

This is where the trouble starts. On the one hand a group of people commit their working lives to expressing in the theatre a view of the world which can't be expressed elsewhere; on the other hand their existence in that world, and their dependence on its material resources for a place to perform and to finance productions, often leads to a compromise with 'respectability'. The great interest in theatre which flowered in the Restoration period after years of suppression, and the continuation of that tradition into the popular forms of the nineteenth century is responsible for both the large number of big, old theatres which still stand today and the reputation they still have for housing something slightly 'scurrilous' and the respectable forum in which it's said. No surprise then that in the middle of the twentieth century the drawing-room should have provided that forum.

The drawing-room comedy

The virtues of the drawing-room comedy within this historical context are several. First, the genre is located in a stratum of society which has been historically important and within which the greatest tensions of our society are experienced – the middle class. While having the wealth and ease to operate freely on its own account, coupled with the education to be informed and articulate, it also has the moral dilemma of either supporting the traditions of the ruling class or of combating them. Second, the drawing-room is a convenient meeting-place for that class and therefore suitable for bringing characters together on stage under realistic circumstances which also strike deep into the roots of personal and family life. Third, since it implies only one set, it is – within the conventions of our old, proscenium-arch theatre buildings – cheap to produce. Fourth, as the meeting-place for the pivotal class in our society, it can also bring working- and ruling-class figures into its action without straining credibility too far. This also makes the thoughts and actions of its characters interesting to sections of the audience drawn from other classes. Both the aristocrat anxious to understand the ways of the rising bourgeoisie, and an educated working-class audience aspiring to middle-class values will find something of interest in the portrayal of its 'drawing-room' manners. Finally, because it stands at a point of tension in British class conflict, it is simultaneously 'respectable' and insecure in its respectability. It can reflect bourgeois values while at the same time criticising them. No wonder then that in its broadest sense it has been our most dominant theatre form – from Shaw through to Ayckbourn.

But the drawing-room has been the dominant context of British theatre not only on stage but also off-stage. To portray a middle-class world is to invite the participation of middle-class practitioners. Writers are said to write best about what they know, and the best actor for a middle-class role would seem to be a middle-class actor. In fact, the class from which most theatre practitioners between the wars were drawn was probably the lower-middle class. Educated enough to appreciate theatre as it was, ambitious enough to join the ranks of the marginally more privileged, but also sufficiently accustomed to poverty to put up with the hardships of theatre at its less illustrious levels, the lower-middle class was the ideal source of manpower. While the upper class dabbled in theatre and the working class tended towards music hall and variety, the lower-middle class gritted its teeth, bore it and hoped for jam tomorrow.

The social context this created meant that not only did this kind of theatre not speak to working-class audiences, it was also virtually closed to working-class practitioners. The few who stayed with it were no doubt soon engulfed by its values and manners. It also meant that wage levels could be held low because the interest of those involved was not primarily financial. They would either suffer gratefully in silence (all part of the mystique, the sense of 'vocation'), or rely on pocket-money from Daddy. When I started work in professional theatre, it was still customary for young acting or assistant stage managers (the traditional bottom rung of the theatre career ladder) to be paid a token wage.

Breaking with tradition

While this remained the dominant form of theatre between the wars, a few serious initiatives did occur to create an alternative to the theatre of this period. The general move towards socialist thinking in the thirties, the Unity theatres and the troupes of Joan Littlewood and Ewan McColl raised the question of a theatre for the people as a whole; but it was a theatre which demanded a different context – different buildings, different audiences, different conventions. The Second World War interrupted the growth of that movement, and by the time it had established a corner of the theatre world for itself, post-war changes in society were already preparing the ground for the next wave.

During the thirties education was seen by many who had no control over industry or government as the best way of building the movement towards socialism. During World War II, when the nation's leaders needed the co-operation of organised labour to defeat Hitler's Germany, a great releasing of social bonds, moral taboos and creative talent took place. Throughout the war, away from their homes, people watched films, listened to concerts, went to lectures, read, talked and learned. The ground-work of the demand for a different kind of culture was already under way.

Every form of theatre is limited historically, but although the changes of post-war subsidised theatre had already rendered the drawing-room comedy 'old hat' by the late sixties, many of the original reasons for its existence – and its sheer suitability for expressing a particular aspect of British society – endured, particularly in the commercial or West End theatre. The general public's image of 'theatre' is still heavily influenced by the traditions of the drawing-room comedy. In setting out to explode those traditions, 'alternative' theatre companies from the late sixties onwards, influenced by both the political and cultural ideas of the 'New Left', opened up the whole question of what theatre is.

2: JUST THEATRE

When we think of theatre, we usually think of a large, public building specially designed – usually with an end-stage and proscenium arch – for audiences to watch actors and actresses perform. But this needn't be the case. Theatre doesn't need a special building. This has been amply demonstrated by those companies who have taken shows out to new audiences in pubs, clubs, public halls and even into streets and parks. Not only this recent work but a brief glimpse at the history of 'popular' theatre in Europe or 'primitive' theatre in other parts of the world will show that it can happen anywhere.

Similarly, it doesn't need to be performed by professionals. The continuous and thriving tradition of 'amateur theatricals' in Britain, the use of untrained and unfamiliar 'faces' in modern cinema, and the charm of children and 'people off the streets' within the framework of a professional production, all point to qualities outside the confines of 'the profession'. Indeed, if one thinks of the *theatrical* rather than just *theatre*, the definition might extend to just one ordinary person getting up to do a turn at a family party, to an animal at the circus, or even to a machine (as at the Planetarium or in Victorian spectacle).

What's more, it needn't necessarily be *plays* that are performed. Theatre will probably involve people moving about and speaking (though one might see Sam Beckett as doing his best to scotch even *that* assumption), but they could also perform a song, a dance, a trick or a joke. The performance could last five seconds or five days, and be with set, costume and props, or without.

Last, there is a sense in which theatre doesn't even need an audience. If we pursue the idea of the *theatrical* it can include someone in the street suddenly bursting into song or doing an impersonation to himself, someone living alone at home and talking to himself or dancing a jig, even to an actor rehearsing alone in an empty auditorium.

Imagination and the 'free zone'

These examples are important because much of the work that goes into theatre – albeit one of the more public and social art forms – is done in isolation. Playwrights generally write alone. Even individuals writing with companies who devise their plays collectively often need to withdraw from the group to get their ideas together on paper. The theatre director may well consider aspects of production – what is required from the actors, how to design, dress and light the show – while alone. Designers usually create their designs while on their own. Even actors, perhaps the most gregarious of theatre workers, have to learn lines and work out an interpretation of their parts *for themselves*. However helpful the director or his colleagues, an actor can't be *made* to act in a certain way simply by being *told*. However great the degree of consultation between the various skills involved, and however much of the production is actually worked out 'on the floor' in rehearsal, pressure is always on the individuals to dredge up creative resources from within their own, personal imaginations. Even rehearsal itself often constitutes a longer period than the hours spent in performance, in front of an audience.

The point here is not that theatre is entirely a thing of the private imagination, but that its creative source for all its practitioners is, inevitably, subjective. Yet the relation between that subjective involvement and the public arena of the stage – where its product is acted out – is very direct. If one could strip away all the social connotations from the space in which theatre is performed, the stage or space itself would be neutral – a potentially free zone in which anything could happen, as untrammelled as our minds and imaginations themselves. Walk into any theatre auditorium when it's totally empty, and the very absence of what usually goes on there holds its own excitement. The potential for free expression is almost palpable. Not only may our minds and imaginations wander freely – as indeed, in moments of relaxation, they may in the world outside the theatre – but here they are expressly encouraged to.

And this was part of the particular attraction of theatre as a medium in the seventies. You didn't have to own a TV station to reach your audience who, in turn, didn't have to own a TV. You weren't controlled by middlemen, you could go anywhere, do anything. The thoughts and feelings generated by the world around you could find their immediate expression in street theatre, pub theatre, a tenants' meeting hall or a converted synagogue.

But part of that sense of freedom is illusory. However freely hearts and minds are stimulated, either by the world in general or by a performance, theatre cannot be entirely divorced from its social context. To begin with, the place where it happens has its own determining character – a fact acknowledged by Peter Cheeseman at Stoke in his insistence on a friendly, familiar atmosphere around the ticket-office and foyer of the Vic. The kind of audience attracted to the work is also a determining factor: how would a working-class audience feel amongst the furs and evening dress of a London first night? However wide a range of 'theatrical' activity is possible, and however private and personal is the engagement of the individuals involved with it, it is obvious that the larger part of theatre production *does* take place in buildings, involves *several* human performers, assumes *professional* standards and at the very least implies an audience, even if no one turns up! This is what determines its quality as one of the more social art forms, and goes a long way to explaining why it has exercised a consistent appeal to those interested in political art. At the same time however, it has remained one of the least innovatory in *form* – certainly compared to twentieth-century developments in music, painting and the novel – which must be due in large part to its production being more socially complex to organise.

Enter the audience

Even if all the physical and material circumstances of production were removed, the outside world would still encroach on that notional freedom of expression in the theatre. Even actors learning lines alone, or people imitating others in the privacy of their homes do so in expectation of some kind of audience function within themselves. They 'perform' to themselves. They step outside 'real' existence for a moment and perform an action which springs from their imagination, but at the same time the 'eye' of their imagination is watching and judging the skill or wit of the action performed. For what is in our minds and imaginations is never entirely original;

conditioned by what has gone before, our 'eye' is trained by the past, even if our conscious stance is total rebellion. Aesthetic sense and taste are *developed* attributes. The moment we approach the stage, whether as audience and critics or as producers, we bring a little of the past with us. However strong our desire as artists towards innovation and experiment, the materials we build with are old ones, and the responses of past audiences remain within us. However powerful and vivid our imaginations, the 'selves' from which we draw are strongly conditioned by what has gone before. A fellow writer once described to me his feelings on starting a new piece of work:

> Every time I start a new play I think this is going to be The Big One, the Play that Says It All, the Great Work of Art. By the time I've finished, put a line under it and written 'The End', I think 'Fuck it, it's me again.'

The same goes for every skill in the theatre.

The product of our minds and imaginations become subject to, as well as a challenge to, the hidden laws of that 'free zone', just as they do in the real world. The moment a character walks on stage, even if it's empty and the character is silent, expectations are aroused – just as in life when someone moves, or opens his mouth to speak. The neutrality is disturbed; that potential freedom has to come to terms with known limits.

Of course, the limits of theatre and of the world outside it are different. Both have the capacity, in one sense at least, to 'contain' the other. Theatre takes place within the physical and economic conditions of the world around it, and is dependent on them for the material resources that make it happen. But theatre is also able to reflect and represent that world within itself. Both can *comment* on the other, but for that comment to become fully effective their distinct and separate laws have to be recognised.

In real life we are directly implicated. If we hit someone, that's a real action and we can expect the real consequences. If someone looks us in the eye and asks us a question, there's no escape, we have to answer. Or if we don't answer, that is significant in itself. Actions are played out inexorably, and even the passive act of being a spectator is significant only in terms of what you're a spectator *of*. The only escape here is into the world of fantasy and the imagination where it's possible to construct a totally different scenario from beginning to end. And in that world of the imagination, spectators are not only significant, they are almost *required*. They keep their distance, but the fact that their minds and imaginations are by definition receptive, that they may be appealed to, is an indispensable part of the exercise.

If I *pretend* to hit someone, even in real life, I make an appeal to that person's function as spectator; I leave that spectator – along with any others watching – to 'complete' the action or relate it back to reality. The consequences of such an action are more varied and unpredictable than a real blow. I might get hit back for real, might be laughed at, simply ignored, or I may succeed in making a point, in 'getting through' to the other person. Although I can't achieve anything *physically*, and my action remains locked in the world of the imagination, its effectiveness *there* can be far greater. The difference between such an action played out in make-believe and the simple comment 'You deserve a punch in the face' is that all the circumstances surrounding the action may also be present. Time, place, climate, people's passions and views may all be presented in our appeal to the mind of the spectator.

We are able to re-create a mini-world of our own with its own rules, and call on all five senses in order to reflect on the real world; but for the actor being watched, this looking-glass world is as inexorable as the real one. His mind may *not* wander. Every action he makes on stage is significant, every question must be answered, and there's no escape except off. I once witnessed a performance where a director stepped in to replace a sick actor, and although he knew the lines, you could see his directorial mind organising the production – his own acting included – as he went along. Far from demonstrating that elusive quality 'presence', he exhuded consummate *absence*. The actor is therefore locked into that imaginary world along with all the other elements of its total vision. These elements together affect how the audience feels about the action represented, along with their will to do anything about its reality. We present a *sense* of the world and hope to impress that sense upon the freely wandering minds and imaginations of our audience.

Laws and effect

Audiences' responses to statements in the theatre frequently operate in a comparable manner to the way the brain 'compensates' for information filtered through the eye. If you see the colour green then close your eyes, your mind's eye sees the colour red. Blue gives orange, and so on. By this analogy a play which loudly proclaims 'Vote Labour' might well send its audience off screaming to the Tories' HQ with offers of money. Spectators can withdraw equally easily from both the real world and the theatre world and are free to respond and comment as they will. Though we can withdraw to the world of the theatre to respond and comment on the real one, that theatre world is not in fact a free one, as actors know only too well. We should be aware of this not only in our creative activity within theatre, but also in our critical activity within and around it. A critical 'note' to an actor only serves the production if it comes in a manner which the actor can take up and use. For the same reason we should also beware of assuming an identity between our comment about the world at large and its expression through the medium of theatre. Talking about art isn't the same as doing it, and just as theatre may reflect on the world but doesn't act on it, so comments from outside the theatre which reflect on its practice remain mere comment until turned into production.

These distinctions are particularly important when discussing a form of theatre with pretensions to social relevance. Too often both practitioners and commentators in the theatre world have assumed an immediate identity between their view of the world, their view of theatre and the expression of those views translated through the medium of an actual theatre piece. They have ignored the fact that in order to be expressed in the world those views have to pass through a variety of different media – books, articles, TV, the stage, even conversation; and because the medium is different each time, the message is also different. The processes that have to be gone through to make a point in conversation, in a reflective piece of writing and in a play, are different, as are the responses of one's reader, audience or fellow conversationalist. In each case someone is transmitting and someone receiving, but as in the game 'Whispers', the message initially transmitted and the one finally received can be very different. This applies as much to discussion about plays – in the process of production (as many Fringe companies have discovered to their cost) as well as in the process of consumption by audiences and critics.

Many Fringe companies have discovered for example that by the time an idea for a play has been first mooted, then discussed three times by the company, then put to a writer, then explained to a director and finally reaches an audience, something entirely different comes out at the other end. What applies to 'transmitters' or producers, of plays also applies to 'receivers': listening to audience discussions after shows or reading a collection of newspaper reviews, I have frequently wondered if people are talking about the same play. Just as hesitation and facial expression can say a lot to a listener in conversation, and style and syntax say a lot to someone reading, so dialogue *and* body language, the whole *being* of an actor are what communicates to an audience in theatre. It's one thing to comment; another thing entirely to *act*.

At the same time, not only actors but everyone connected with the making of a piece of theatre, in the very process of communicating about their work, commits a little of their person to it. New plays from writers which seem opaque on the page can suddenly become clear (and sometimes misleadingly) when the company meets the writer in person. A great many of the clues which actors pick up from directors are communicated through the director's personality. A set design may seem dead on paper but begins to make sense when one talks to its creator. The business of crystallising the content of one's work in theatre is finally achieved not by description but by action. This makes the circumstances of actual production an extremely important element in what a piece of theatre eventually communicates to its audience. Given the radical changes in production process embarked on by alternative theatre companies and the huge variety in their organisational structures, these questions have been a further contributory factor to the lack of cohesion and definition in the community theatre movement. The theatre world has been confused with the real world. Imaginative thought has been confused with critical thought. People's personalities have become totally confused with their function within the production process. Form has been mistaken for content, intent for effect. Some theatre workers in the seventies came close to behaving as though the work of their companies could lead a revolution single-handed; others as though *they* were the working class. Certain kinds of political consciousness led people to confuse the tenets of political organisation with the organisation of a theatre company. Politically conscious criticism of society was confused with its representation on stage.

As a consequence many observers and critics of their work also became confused, identifying poor theatre with poor politics and vice-versa. The truth is more complex. While good politics sometimes made lousy theatre, and the best theatre frequently made lousy politics, there were also from time to time glimpses of a profoundly different and successful relation between the two; because of the very concrete nature of theatre production and its social complexity, part of the clue to understanding this relation lies in a close examination of the production process in contemporary theatre through which it was happening.

3: HOW THEATRE IS MADE

If the game of 'Whispers' indicates some of the dangers inherent in the production system of collective theatre companies, 'Pass the Parcel' is the game most analogous to production in conventional theatre. The system by which plays are produced in both the West End and the larger subsidised houses, though widely accepted as the norm, is in fact limited historically and has evolved exclusively within the context of a predominantly 'free' market economy. As with any enterprise in such an economy, the 'floating' of a new product is dependent on the raising of initial capital and the subsequently successful selling of that product in the market-place. This method, and the motivations associated with it, will remain dominant in any field of production until or unless state subsidy intervenes on a sufficiently significant scale to alter it radically. Theatre in a predominantly 'free' economy – even theatre on the smallest scale and of the most virulently anti-capitalist kind – is no exception to this rule. Whatever its content, theatre constitutes an expensive 'package' (a term used, revealingly, more and more these days) to put together. A script has to be procured, director and designer engaged, set and costumes made, actors and technicians hired, rehearsal and performance space found and paid for, publicity got out and the smooth administration of the whole operation ensured. All this before a penny changes hands at the box-office.

In the mixed economy of a welfare state with partial subsidy of the arts, it is of course possible to set this process in motion with help from the arts-funding bodies, or (as frequently happened in the seventies) by people living on the dole, or doing part-time work and, in effect, subsidising the work themselves. Even if a theatre product is floated without private capital, its relationship to the public is still ultimately governed by the same financial considerations which affect every aspect of our lives. Subsidy in Britain is only partial and while it may reduce seat-prices slightly, it is certainly not sufficient to effect any radical, qualitative change in the relationship between producers and audience. The dole or part-time jobs are no way to sustain a consistent and continuous programme of artistic work, and even if you were able to present the occasional show free of charge, the box-office would still finally be your principal source of income. This means that the box-office effectively becomes the most important material link between producers and consumers. It bridges the gap between the two sides of the operation and inevitably dictates that there has to be an element of 'selling' if there is to be any return on the initial investment, whether that investment be of private money, public subsidy or labour freely donated by the individuals involved.

The parcel game
Presiding over this operation there has to be some kind of producing management

with either a script or an idea for a show, and often with a director already involved. In commercial theatre, as in the film industry, this 'property' often arrives with the producer in a brown paper envelope, and once he 'buys' it (either literally or metaphorically – again a revealing usage), the process gets under way. If money needs to be raised, as in the commercial or West End theatre, the script is once again wrapped up in a brown paper envelope and sent out to financial backers or 'angels' as they're sometimes, not uncynically, called. Depending on the backers' confidence in the likely box-office success of the 'package', and their consequent enthusiasm for it, more or less money will be raised. By this time the brown paper envelope may also have been sent to a director and leading actors whose interest in working on the package will increase (or detract from) its attraction as a financial proposition. At each stage of this initial process a certain amount of 'selling' has to accompany the passing round of the 'package' in order to bring all the necessary parties together and 'bridge the gap' between them as well. Finally it's sent out to a designer and further actors, and once sufficient publicity to catch the public's attention has gone out, the packaging is complete.

All this can happen before a single word is exchanged on the rehearsal floor, the actual 'factory' where the product is made, and where so many decisions affecting the actual quality of the eventual product will be taken. On the first day of perhaps only three weeks' rehearsal, a group of people from perhaps widely dispersed homes, of different incomes, ages and beliefs, possibly never having met each other before, come together with only one thing in common: they all carry an identical brown paper envelope under their arms. During the weeks that follow they will strip it away layer by layer – and in the process quite possibly strip away layers from themselves as well and then finally dress themselves and its contents up again for sale on the first night of performance. How will it look when it's finished? How do the people involved feel about it? Will they all get on with each other? Do they know what they're getting involved in?

No one actually knows yet what's in the parcel, but accompanying music makes sure that no one lingers over it too long to peek inside. That music is the confidence and enthusiasm which is whipped up as it passes from hand to hand. As with any business enterprise, it's crucial that the initial 'selling' of the idea behind it is achieved with as much confidence and apparent enthusiasm as possible. In theatre that enthusiasm ought to be a natural by-product of the creative process under any system of production. But in the 'parcel game' it frequently emanates originally from one or two individuals only, and in the very act of buying and selling an idea, a division between the two sides to the transaction is created and emphasised. It's in the nature of good ideas that they inspire confidence and enthusiasm; but it's in the nature of *selling* ideas that they can't be seen to be anything but 'good'. Consequently all ideas for shows that go into production have to be assumed to be good – at least to start with.

How can you know for sure? It's easy enough to weed out a really bad script, but it's rare for even an experienced theatre director to read a script and predict exactly how it'll work on stage. Impresarios and producers seldom have much profound insight into the practical process of transition from page to stage. For actors, whose principal consideration is necessarily the part they are being asked to consider, the task is even more difficult. From the word go, the process is insecure. Judgements about productions are consequently made much more frequently on the basis of reputation, track record, gossip and hearsay than on the actual and immediate qualities of the script or personnel involved. If an author has had a past success with a similar play, or an actor has previously been good in a similar part, these are grounds enough for confidence – even if, for example, the differences this time are more crucial than the similarities. Under this system, superficial qualities – the 'wrapping' – are more important than the goods inside. A package can be sold provided a sufficient number of known reference points can be mustered to establish its sales potential.

This is obviously important in commercial theatre if the initial investment is to be recouped; but within this whole 'sales pitch' someone could be lying, or misguided. The person whose initial enthusiasm kicked the process off could be feathering his own nest at the expense of the others involved. Built into the need to sell a show, whether to fellow theatre workers or to the general public, is the possibility of coercion into a bad cause. In the commercial theatre of course, a show doesn't necessarily have to be good, it just has to 'do well'. Whatever the content of the parcel, provided it is wrapped in the shiniest, brightest, most colourful packaging available, the belief is that it will 'get across' – as if the row of footlights separating audience from actors were somehow a physical manifestation of sales resistance.

Many actors see the business of 'getting it across' or 'making it work' or 'putting it over' as their sole function, as if they were dragging an immovable object over a bottomless chasm, engineers renovating a long broken-down machine, or con-men duping their prey. However much these attitudes have developed as a consequence of long and painful experience at doing something very similar with intractable material on numerous occasions, the paradox remains that someone specifically *chose* that material, and *belief* in it still remains paramount. It's even possible – if the money, working conditions and the companionship of other actors are good enough – for wilful self-deception about the quality of the work to continue right to the end of the run. Only in retrospect will an actor then acknowledge, 'Yes, actually it was a load of rubbish.'

Next job syndrome

So, in spite of the razzamatazz and the very *need* for belief in the material, the element of doubt is never far away. Is the script really likely to be popular? Is the director really the best person for the job? Have the leading actors really been chosen for their suitability, or simply for their ability to pull a crowd? These doubts – a product of the gap between the production's artistic needs and the sales-led thinking of a management operating in a 'free' market – can make for further divisions amongst the individuals involved in the production. In the commercial theatre these divisions can be largely responsible for the qualities of nervousness, competitiveness and rank individualism associated with it. Is the author actually a cretin? Has the director got the guts to cope with these temperamental stars? Will they upstage me? Will my performance be good enough to make sure I get asked again to do another play?

The hope that one will be 'asked again' verges on being a chronic condition for actors. Given the scarcity of jobs in the theatre, it's no surprise that it frequently leads to that other, allied complaint, 'Next Job Syndrome', where a performance is given principally with an eye to the next part the actor would *really* like to play. For it would be a mistake to imagine that once rehearsals begin, the outside world is locked out completely, that the goods inside the 'package' aren't subject to the same market pressures which surrounded its being put together in the first place. People do not stop living in the world at large just because they're working on a play; and that part of them which is needed for the package to be marketable is neither their whole being nor even necessarily the part of them which they hope to satisfy in the world of theatre.

Everyone working on the production is also operating as an individual within the same market that the production is hoping to conquer; but not everyone's interest in the production will be identical, nor will their attitude towards that market. They are 'being used' (what happens after you've 'been asked') for this show but, unlike the exploitation of labour in other contexts, there is also a sense in which they can use the show to serve their own individual ends. While it's usually in everyone's interest to maintain the traditional belief in the job in hand, the element of doubt can always reassert itself. If, for example, it appears that the show may well turn out to be a disaster, the customary concentration and commitment which actors give can disappear faster than rats off a sinking ship. To be identified with a flop is bad enough; to be *seen* to be identifying with it is far worse. In an insecure profession where jobs are scarce, good jobs scarcer, and above all where one is required to be totally and personally involved, this is no surprise. But the 'Next Job Syndrome' goes further.

For everyone working in theatre there is a profound sense that the work one is doing at present is only a stepping-stone towards something better. The Great Work of Art, the Big One which says it all, the Play To End All Plays, is only just around the corner. This has as much to do with the restlessness of an artistic temperament as it has with crass ambition. Very few people in show business are totally content with what they're doing at any given moment. This applies as much to the long-running West End hit or TV sit-com which they're 'only doing for the money' as to unpaid work in a dingy cellar on the Fringe. Even a long-term contract at the National or RSC, with security of employment and the chance to do a range of interesting parts, leaves many actors feeling dissatisfied.

It was this dissatisfaction, coupled with the confidence in their own abilities and judgement generated by the buoyant culture of the sixties, which prompted many theatre workers in the seventies not to wait to 'be asked' but to 'do it themselves' and to 'do it now'. This was not only a response to the kind of work being offered in conventional theatre, but also to the overall quality of communication with the public which theatre as a whole was offering at that time. Instead of a system where a number of people have collective access to social wealth and jointly decide how it shall be used to communicate with that audience, you had – and in conventional theatre still have – a series of individual initiatives, each of whose ultimate criterion has to be a financially successful product. Instead of the joy of collaborative and creative effort, there is the anxiety of competitiveness. At each stage of a show's development, from the initial hiring of performers through rehearsal to the first night and beyond, doubts about the 'success' of the play will never be entirely dispelled, nor will the nervous, defensive reflexes associated with that doubt. Since each particular skill contributing to the production in hand also has an eye to its own interests within the broader market, traditional defences have built up to preserve those interests.

I'm all right, Jack . . .

Apart from the much joked-about desire of actors to upstage each other (in Britain, paradoxically, the humbler the production, the less common this is), the principal clash of wills in theatre production is between the actor who needs guidance from the director to make a part 'his own' and the director who needs performances from actors which will add up to his 'own' interpretation of the play as a whole. Alongside this clash, but usually on the sidelines, is the playwright hoping like mad that the performance which comes out of all this is his 'own' play. It's quite possible, for example, if actors change writers' lines, whether consciously or unconsciously, for the writer to be accredited with them (for better or worse) by a reviewer. Similarly 'selfish' motives can operate for the other skills involved. If a set design is to look good in production, the designer needs a decent budget. With a decent budget it's possible to give both set and costume an impressive and coherent visual style. It's quite possible however for a visually impressive set to be totally impractical for actors to move around on, or for visually impressive costumes to be impossible to move around *in*. Some of the best features of set design – as with a director's 'interpretation' – are therefore *invisible*. Reviewers who only comment favourably on impressive design and interpretation (which may have caused havoc for the acting company) do not necessarily do the business a great service.

These defensive reflexes can be compounded. Directors in the theatre are responsible for the co-ordination of all the different skills involved and learn to cope with their interplay in order to steer the production towards a cohesive whole. Budget limits are set, have generally to be adhered to closely, and within this context a director may be coping with highly temperamental, apparently egocentric and certainly specialised interests. The worst directors learn to manipulate these elements only in order to defend and retain their overall control. The best find ways of channelling the variety and potential on offer in order to assemble the most satisfying creative product for everyone. While directors constantly give everyone else feedback, it's very rare that anyone gives them any. It can be an extremely lonely job, and because the interest of different skills may clash, no director is blameless in everyone's eyes. If, for example, a director wished to restrain over-reaching ambition in a designer, he might well decide to limit the design budget. But with a limited budget, a special item of costume which could add a decisive dimension to an actor's interpretation of a part, could be lost for ever. This is one of the ways in which the use of money as a means of maintaining 'discipline' can be artistically destructive. But so closely connected are the considerations of the market and of one's 'image' that the same destructive effect can be achieved without money even being mentioned. It's possible, for example, to employ an actor or a designer for, say, a naturalistic play on the grounds that they've done this kind of work well before, but for the person engaged to be suffering from a reputation (from reviewers or within the business as a whole) for 'always being boringly naturalistic'. The consequence might well be for that person to rebel and direct their energies against the entire grain of the production.

In this way, divisions of interest grow up between the different skills involved in a production. If these conflicting interests remain focussed on the job in hand, they can provide a productive tension. If not, they become a serious distraction. Similar divisions of interest exist in any walk of life and are present in the field of subsidised theatre as well, but they can be greatly exacerbated in the commercial sector. Everyone involved, if not in fact 'selling' themselves, is contained within a market where *not* to do so, in the short term at least, puts you at a disadvantage. This means that the quiet, solid, unflashy skills which hold together the theatre's collaborative processes either go completely unrecognised or take longer to establish themselves. Within a permanent company these effects can be minimised, but where people are hired on a once-off basis, these dangers will always prevail. The show has one chance only, and for the people working on it – with all their different interests and ambitions – the show is just one opportunity to prove not only that they can do *this* job but that they can do *the* job.

It is of course possible for individual managements and directors, particularly in the subsidised sector, to moderate the worst effects of the parcel game. Except for the rare case of the totally autocratic director whose ideas about a show are so rigidly formulated that he believes he requires no stimulus from his colleagues – or indeed ignores or crushes all other creative contributions – it's not unusual for first the director, writer and designer, then these together with the whole company to plan and share the concept of a production together. Then the 'natural' collaborative spirit of theatre work comes into play and the director becomes less of a 'boss', more of a co-ordinator.

But even in the subsidised sector the same underlying pressures obtain. In a large subsidised company, running five or six plays in repertory, for example, it's possible for the general manager's pocket calculator to decide a production should be dropped and a new production brought forward, and for the acting company suddenly to find their work-load increased by twenty per cent. Where productions in different auditoria are 'paired' against each other so that the same actors can play different shows on different nights, this sort of rescheduling can lead to directors competing desperately for available actors, and actors walking around with seven plays in their heads. Under these conditions, if there is financial difficulty or a clash of personalities, the collaborative spirit can quickly be broken. At this point the formal system comes into play, and everyone goes home to look up their contracts. The major victims of these clashes are invariably those furthest removed from the managerial hub – sometimes the writer or designer but most frequently the actors or technicians. The technicians' trades unions are traditionally better at defending their members' interests (generally considered to be purely functional, though this needn't be the case), so it is most often the actors who have to bear the main brunt of a breakdown in the 'parcel game' system.

. . . but what about 'Them'?

The audience of course shares none of these concerns. It is only interested in the one show it has bought a ticket for. It is *this* show which is required to fulfil all its expectations of what theatre is, not the 'next job' which the professionals are interested in. Yet again there is a division of interest. The audience, has, effectively, bought the whole package with all the internal conflicts and divisions it contains and, most significantly, the effect of those divisions on the product itself. Since neither the aspirations of those involved in production nor the expectations of the audience are being fully addressed, it's no surprise that the experience is rarely satisfactory.

It is of no concern to an audience whether budgets were sufficient, whether the director was more interested in the television play he was doing next, whether the designer was having an affair with the leading actress, or whether everyone came down with flu for the dress rehearsal. Similarly it is of no concern to the producing company whether this particular show measured up to how the audience had interpreted Jan Kott on Shakespeare, Esslin on Brecht or John Russell Taylor on Pinter. And since a show can 'do well' without being good, even good box-office receipts are no satisfactory criterion of success. One discontented member of the audience can be enough to depress an actor for a week. On the other hand public taste is notorious for lagging behind the most progressive work. Even the judgement of professional reviewers generally falls into a narrow consensus defined by the ownership of newspapers and, one imagines, the dinner party circuit within the London Borough of Camden. The standards by which contemporary theatre is judged are confused and, at times, quite contradictory. When the Arts Council, in deliberating about subsidy, makes reference to these 'standards', the hilarity with which this is greeted in the profession is only marred by the apprehension that it might be one's own guffaws which its random axe next cuts short.

So when an actor is 'asked' to do a show, who is actually doing the asking? Ultimately, we would all like to think, the public. In the case of a commercial production mounted around the name of a celebrated writer, actor or director, there is perhaps an argument for saying that the public really is 'asking' for the product. But already we are being trapped into 'package' thinking. That 'name' is yet another wrapping in the parcel game which conceals a working artist with his or her own vision, ambition and taste. There is no guarantee that a successful author will want to repeat the formula that worked before, or that a celebrated actor isn't sick to the back teeth of doing the same old stuff he's always done; a performance your heart isn't in is not a recipe for success.

One of the most serious dangers for contemporary theatre is that its writers, actors and directors end up working with an eye to how managements interpret their audiences' tastes rather than to audiences themselves. This must be a considerable factor in the dwindling popularity of theatre, and it is even more pronounced in the subsidised field where the absolute necessity of taking the audience into account is not so great. All artists long for the opportunity and control which would bring them the freedom to express themselves totally. But many artistic directors are so hell-bent on seizing that opportunity, they forget their audience completely. Those seeking work from the same artistic director are more likely to trim their talents to fit in with that individual director's concerns than with their sense of the audience's.

Compare these systems of judging 'what the public wants' with the enormously successful series of television plays, *Boys from the Blackstuff*. It's doubtful that the name of Alan Bleasdale, his director or any of the actors involved in those plays could have pulled a West End audience, but given the existing production structure of BBC TV drama and a certain captive audience, the possibility existed for a play to catch the spirit of its time totally, to reach millions of people directly experiencing its subject – unemployment – in a way which was entertaining yet also spoke for a certain dignity in an economic climate where dignity is a very rare commodity. Even then the public didn't, literally, ask for it.

The truth is that it is those who control the means of producing and distributing our culture who make the choices 'on behalf', as it were, of their audience. Yet however great their expertise at divining popular taste, they are still in some sense dependent on 'selling' their product. *Boys from the Blackstuff* didn't need to be sold in quite that way. Maybe the original idea for it had initially to be 'sold' to the Head of Drama, maybe it helped to have it prominently advertised in the *Radio Times* and through advance trailers on TV itself; but in those instances the basic content of the show, its central interest for an audience was, we assume, already secure. The product was not created on the basis of marketability, but did subsequently discover a 'market'.

In the West End or commercial theatre, given the huge amounts of money that need to be raised prior to production, and given that it is a once-off event with no context of a captive audience or permanent production back-up, a show *does* need to be sold before it's created. It could be argued that live theatre is such a minority interest these days that such selling is necessary. Even then it remains, in artistic as well as financial terms, enormously risky. It could also be argued that this way of looking at theatre belongs basically to the nineteenth century, and only receives pure expression in the West End, which is in its death-throes anyway. But so dominant is the need to 'sell' a piece of theatre, and so prevalent are the safety mechanisms of the theatre workers hired as its salesmen, that the same reflexes have come to operate even in the subsidised field where, in theory at least, the pressure to 'sell' the product shouldn't be so great. But with levels of subsidy so low, and the Arts Council's consequent insistence that companies 'earn their keep', the same reflexes and motivations have come to be reproduced even in the subsidised sector.

4: THE INFLUENCE OF SUBSIDY

With the Labour landslide government at the end of World War II, strong agitation within the profession, alongside the example of the wartime Council for the Encouragement of Music and the Arts and educational programmes for the troops, led to the creation of the Arts Council of Great Britain with a view to providing art for 'the mass of the population'. Throughout the fifties and sixties much of the effort by progressive people in the theatre went into setting up national and regional theatres, subsidised by the Arts Council, with the aim of broadening the social class composition of audiences, making the general fare at our theatres more serious, and following the example of France, Germany and other European countries with a longer tradition of subsidy for cultural and intellectual life. Stephen Joseph's Theatre-in-the-Round at Scarborough, Peter Cheeseman's Victoria Theatre at Stoke-on-Trent, Joan Littlewood's Theatre Royal at Stratford East, George Devine's Royal Court and Peter Hall's Royal Shakespeare Company were all part of this movement. Even the 100-year-old dream of a National Theatre was revived.

Plus ça change

But while these initiatives were taking place within the *theatre*, the troops were all going back to *work*. The women who'd worked during the war went back to housewifery, and the teachers back to the schools and universities. By the time the struggle for a serious subsidised theatre had resolved itself into the mixed-economy, semi-subsidised theatre we have now, the 'mass of the population' were once more locked up in their homes, doing-it-themselves, improving their furniture and . . . watching TV. The people and the live art they now paid for through their taxes were still as far apart as in the heyday of drawing-room comedy. In fact the working class was now subsidising middle-class audiences.

Just as the nationalisation of coal and steel effected only a slight change in the lives of miners and steelworkers, so subsidy in the theatre of the fifties and sixties did little to change the basic relations of production inherited from pre-war commercial theatre.

The degree of danger and risk in these relations is obvious and, indeed, is part of the very excitement of show business, but for those whose money is being spent, whether 'angels' or the tax-paying public, the tension is of a different kind. They want to be certain that this potentially explosive situation, riddled with doubt and anxiety, is policed and its risks are minimised. The producing management is required to ensure watertight contracts with its employees dealing with every eventuality; to procure scripts for as small an advance payment and as small a royalty percentage of the box-office takings as possible; to pay the actors, traditionally, less for a 6-8 hour rehearsal day than for a 2-4 hour performance day; to keep set, props and costume –

even the number of actors engaged – to the absolute minimum. It is rare these days for a large-cast, spectacular, musical show to be mounted in either the commercial or the subsidised theatre. The two-character play on a bare stage isn't the Theatre of the Absurd or 'searing psychological drama', it's the theatre of advanced capitalist crisis. Never mind the dozens of once-necessary skills (dressers, sempstresses, carpenters, painters) now no longer needed and whose ghosts picket the stage door, tensions here and now on the rehearsal floor can upset the applecart of even this attenuated form of theatre. But these risks are a *consequence* of this method of production, and in the commercial theatre it falls to the director to keep those skills being used in harmonious co-operation. He is, as it were, the management's foreman on the rehearsal floor. The success of the production will depend as much on his handling of 'personnel' problems as any artistic inspiration he brings to bear.

The artistic director
In the subsidised field, although it is public money which floats the operation, the relationship between management and hired theatre workers is structurally identical. Instead of an impresario or producer managing the private investment of individual backers, a theatre board presides over the management of public investment provided by the 'mass of the population'. This board usually comprises local politicians, academics and churchmen, plus the occasional 'expert' from the profession. Appointment is often within the gift of local bodies, but, as with the Arts Council itself, there is no direct representation or accountability. Day-to-day management falls to the artistic director, a job in which many of the functions of a producer are telescoped together with that of director. However, the board's right arm (frequently hung perilously close to the artistic director's windpipe) is more likely to be the administrator or general manager of the theatre, whose principal task is to ensure that the financial consequences of the reputedly 'wayward' artists' operations are not disastrous. But far from being responsible for just one production, artistic directors are responsible for whole seasons at a time, for the actual artistic policy of the theatre, including the hiring of their fellow artists.

This division of administrative responsibility into its artistic and financial components can work if it is accompanied by mutual trust and understanding, but the very opposition of the two functions can set them at loggerheads. In Britain, if there is a choice to be made between art and money, money always prevails. The consequence is that our regional subsidised theatres, overseen by generally philistine boards, have come to earn a reputation for safe, middle-of-the-road theatre which will guarantee the sixty-per-cent box-office capacity approved by the Arts Council (who must admit their own responsibility in this). Identikit seasons of plays emerge from these subsidy-prisons: one Shakespeare, one Restoration comedy, one Chekhov or Ibsen (or possibly Arthur Miller, Tennessee Williams – foreign at any rate), one slightly more obscure classical play (usually one that's recently been revived by the National or RSC), one 'modern' play (yet another production of *Godot*, or *The Caretaker*, or perhaps a Stoppard or an Ayckbourn), one 'old favourite' like *Charley's Aunt*, a Ben Travers farce, an Agatha Christie or a Priestley, the Christmas panto and one other.

This 'one other' is often as much scope as the artistic director gets to develop an individual policy. Occasionally it's a new play, but since new plays tend to sink without trace amongst the brand-names on these cultural supermarkets' shelves, artistic directors have a hard time 'selling' them to their boards. In fact, where seasons of new plays have been vigorously implemented, they have frequently done better business and revived local interest in theatre as a whole. Since Peter Cheeseman pioneered the local documentary in the sixties, something similar has often been favourite for this slot, when it was observed that local audiences who didn't usually come to the theatre might actually turn out to see a piece of their own history. This is as close, in terms of content at least, as most subsidised, regional theatres ever got to the idea of community theatre. With the local documentary, at least some working-class taxpayers were reclaiming part of their culture. It also appeared at a time when the first sons and daughters educated by the welfare state were approaching adulthood, and for many of them no doubt it acted as a model which made some sense of the confused values of this mixed cultural economy.

But whatever the sop to the artistic director's personal vision (and some preferred the Theatre of the Absurd, the Theatre of Cruelty, Brecht, Grotowski or to lure a well-known London playwright to the regions), the battle with the board and the huge burden of administrative work often made the job unpalatable. All one really controlled was not the artistic side of the job but the employment of one's fellow artists – an invidious position for anyone. Directors are perhaps more used to this function, which may explain why they comprise ninety per cent of artistic directors, though I have yet to hear a satisfactory explanation of why they, as opposed to actors, writers or technicians, are assumed to be more suitable. Certainly, since the opportunity directly to develop an *artistic* policy is so hedged around in these circumstances, the job could be done by anyone with a modicum of administrative sense. In fact, the job amounts to little more than an updated version of its fore-runner, the actor-manager. Indeed, one of the most successful artistic directors of the sixties, who for a while generated a remarkable civic awareness of culture, was the actor John Neville, in Nottingham.

As a consequence of the meagre artistic opportunities the job offers, many of our most imaginative directors left to work abroad in the sixties, or went into television. Similarly, many talented, though not commercially successful, writers (James Saunders, John Arden, Edward Bond) were produced more abroad than at home or also looked to the opportunities of television (David Mercer, John McGrath, Trevor Griffiths). For actors like Tom Courtenay, Albert Finney, Glenda Jackson, David Warner, the cinema offered the most exciting prospects. The dead hand of civic management had chosen a new breed of foremen to watch over the public's purse-strings – a breed of mainly middle-class, university-educated young men, who became trapped in the managerial problems before their creative ideals could even emerge.

The insulated theatre

By the late sixties the steam had slready gone out of the subsidised regional theatre renaissance. The initiatives of Jennie Lee's arts ministry were already foundering on the rocks of the new 'parcel game' generated by the mixed economy. Frustrated in their desire to produce 'serious' theatre, the new breed of artistic directors, insulated from crude market pressure (and therefore also from a popular audience), put much of their remaining energy into rather erudite productions of the classics and unfamiliar, up-market new work which, if it didn't do good box-office would at least receive a nod of informed approval from 105 Piccadilly (the home of the Arts Council). Beckett and Pinter were then mysterious to their audiences. The theatre gained a reputation as a place to be puzzled in. The fashion was for plays with inconclusive endings – even on television. The gap between practitioners and audience was as large as ever. The sales pitch now, since no one was really sure about the content, was through style. Stoppard, Pinter, Beckett became brand-names whereby, if you weren't sure about the contents, at least you could tell what you were getting by the wrapper. 'Beckettian' and 'Pinteresque' became terms by which you recognised cheap imitations. Ever since Ken Tynan went out on a limb for Osborne in the *Observer* and Harold Hobson for Pinter in the *Sunday Times*, the 'serious' reviewers have had to cover the flank of the sophisticated, 'knowing' section of their readership, and consequently have seen nothing but emperors' new clothes. For as soon as a product breaks through the market's defences and the bandwagon begins to roll, it's a serious offence to be left off it. Once the product is on GCE syllabuses and is studied in universities, it becomes a 'market leader'. It *will* put bums on sixty per cent of seats because the University/Sunday paper/NW3 consensus (collectively a sort of cultural *Which* magazine) has deemed it a 'good buy'.

But the money people were paying at the box-office no longer related to the real price. Consequently society's sense of its value and importance was also diminished. The whole exercise became insulated, distant, artificial. Audiences divided into the enthusiasts who didn't mind and took advantage of artificially depressed prices, and those who did and stayed away. Instead of new initiatives to reach out to those who stayed away, the gains that had been made were preserved. The subsidised theatre fell back on the lessons of the commercial theatre. Commercial theatre even began to revive by using its private capital jointly with public resources in try-outs at subsidised theatres. These exercises generally redounded more to the credit and advantage of the West End than the subsidised sector.

Just as government intervention in industry had succeeded only in shoring up ailing private enterprise, so subsidised theatre became the captive once again of the 'free market'. Instead of being an integral part of its audience's lives, current efforts to make theatre part of people's 'life-style', by the very nature of the inducements offered, demonstrate that the gap is wider than ever: season tickets, tickets for shows and meals combined, two for the price of one, even packages including a trip to London with the show thrown in. Only by *intervening* in people's lives, by battering audience passivity, by making it more expensive for those people who still want to go to the theatre of their choice, followed by the restaurant of their choice, alone or accompanied as they please and *not* carrying a day's shopping, can you sell the product. The question that the product, or the method of making it, might be wrong never seems to occur.

The system is harder to challenge than it was before. Where once a failed artistic enterprise went to the wall, the great milch-cow at 105 Piccadilly can now save it. The value-system of semi-subsidised theatre is well protected by the network of relations established by those within its cocoon: from 105 Piccadilly out to the Regional Arts Associations; to the arts administrators who can work equally easily for the theatre companies as for the funding bodies; to the artistic directors; to the writers successfully manipulating the Arts Council's arcane Writing Schemes; to the reviewers whose standing with all these is as important as their standing with their editors; to the publishers who can't afford to publish unless a play is produced by a 'national' company; to the universities who don't know plays exist till they're in print; to the audiences who don't go unless this consensus tells them to. No wonder that, faced with the impossibility of further growth through the subsidised system, much of Joan Littlewood's mature work found its way into the West End. No wonder that Belt and Braces and the Half Moon are travelling the same road in the eighties. To imagine however that these popular successes 'give the public what it wants', or that these individual initiatives are solving the problem of the faults in the structure, is to ignore all the lessons of the 'parcel game'. The totalitarianism of the 'market leader', with its emphasis on either the rarefied consensus of the cultural elite, or the crude; immediate simplicities of popular iconoclasm, is as rigid as that of political censorship in Eastern Europe. If the market doesn't get you, then the Party will.

5: THE FRINGE-SAMIZDAT OF THE WEST

The belief that *samizdat*, the circulation of 'unofficial' literature in the Soviet Union, is a phenomenon unique to Eastern Europe requires somewhat closer scrutiny. Since access to the means of publication in Eastern Europe is largely controlled by a fairly tight network of publishers and Writers Union officials, themselves largely controlled by the Party, there inevitably exists a kind of 'in crowd', with a fairly common understanding of what it's acceptable to publish within their society. For some of this 'in crowd', one may suppose, this understanding is genuinely a matter of principle. For others, consciously or unconsciously, it is a matter of self-interested expediency –whether with a view to getting ahead in their careers, enjoying popularity amongst their peers, or to leading a relatively comfortable and undisturbed life. These are all thoroughly human, if not particularly heroic, qualities. Though they are officially unacknowledged within communist society (in spite of the advancement they can bring), they are freely acknowledged – if not positively encouraged – in the more open, pluralist West. Indeed, in the 'hard times' of the recession-ridden eighties at least, it has become virtually a mark of intelligence to 'look after Number One'.

When one looks, however, at the number of small magazines, fringe and touring theatre companies, community newspapers and local video groups which have existed in this country since the late sixties without (too much) harrassment but also without growth, the importance of large-scale capital for the development of artistic endeavour, whether private or state capital, becomes evident. When one looks at those who manage that capital in our own theatre managements, arts-funding bodies, publishing houses and national newspapers, heroism is not the first quality that springs to mind. Furthermore, when one looks at the actions, motives and consensus among them concerning what is 'acceptable' within our society, the idea of an 'in crowd' of cultural time-servers no longer appears such an exclusively East European phenomenon.

What also emerges from the comparison, however, is that in both societies two constants govern the production of art: first, that you cannot prevent people saying what's on their mind simply by closing the principal channels of communication to them; second, that artists in any society will inevitably work either through or around the channels that are available. Whether working under a capitalist or under a state-subsidised system, the divide between originating artists and their public is as wide as ever. The sense of artists 'belonging' to their community or of the community having their 'own' artists remains a distant prospect. These are important points when considering the birth and development of fringe and community theatre from the late sixties through to the present day, for it was the very 'corporate' nature of the Establishment's ideological control over the nation's cultural resources in the ways I've indicated above, which forced people to break away and 'do their own thing' in the sixties, and it is the failure of those initiatives to achieve a sufficiently powerful foothold in the cultural fabric of the country which has kept them peripheral.

Out of the drawing-room into the parlour

If the model play of the commercial theatre between the wars was the middle-class, drawing-room comedy, the model play of the semi-subsidised fifties and sixties was the lower-middle-class, living-room drama. Whatever went on in it, be it the sexual hypocrisy in Joe Orton's work, the psychological power-games in Harold Pinter's, or the socially frustrated *cris de coeur* of John Osborne, quite a few thoroughly English, theatrical criteria, inherited from the commercial tradition, survived. First, they were nearly all proscenium-arch, box-set shows; second, they were all set within, maintained and depended on a peculiarly English social veneer – the commonly understood and brittle politenesses of a 'respectable' life-style which they all sought by one means or another to transcend. In all of these plays a 'norm' of English social existence had to be set up in order to be shot down. That norm was demonstrated frequently through 'normal' conversation, under which lurked deeper and thoroughly unrespectable passions. This provided the dramatic tension to these plays, and its articulation in many cases was, paradoxically, through the inarticulacies of colloquial speech. Language became the arena in which conflicts were fought out, through which shifts of mood and motivation were indicated and which, by virtue of being the arena itself, invariably ended up unable to resolve the conflict. In Orton and Pinter it was an unspoken (!) rule that what went unsaid was more important than what was said. Even with writers like Osborne and Wesker, who were capable of putting extraordinarily impassioned and articulate expression into their characters' mouths, it was often the moments when they fell silent that spoke loudest. The other common factor amongst these plays, important as a distinction from what came after, was that however positively and self-consciously the writers, directors and actors of that period saw their involvement in these plays as a 'movement' away from the mainstream tradition, and however much its writers came to see their 'realism' as a trap to struggle away from, they still operated within the traditional system of production.

On each of these fronts – traditional buildings and audience-actor relations, the aesthetics of plays whose *verbal* qualities were all-important, the hierarchical hire-and-fire system of production – the 'fringe' generation from the late sixties onwards chose to take up an oppositional stance. Liberal educational values, the loosening of many social and sexual attitudes, the tide of a new politics in the late sixties, and the very advances already made by the previous generation in theatre encouraged people to go a step further. In examining the consistency of the steps that were taken, it's perhaps sensible to keep each aspect of that opposition distinct from the others.

The pros-arch prison

The similarity between a proscenium-arch stage and a shop window is not accidental. The goods behind it remain passively contained on display while the onlooker decides to take or leave them as he pleases. But once the confines of passive display are accepted, the actor assumes a great measure of freedom and power within them. The acceptance that what takes place on stage is distinct and separate from real life lends its actions the freedom to be as preposterous or outrageous as it wishes. It also lends to the subjective will of the actor the power temporarily to dominate his audience's imagination. This licence to 'dress up' the goods, even to go 'over the top', is all part of the process of objectification implied by an end-stage, proscenium-arch audience-actor relationship. It magnifies the separation between audience and actor and sets them up as adversaries. It also sharpens any predisposition to aggression which either party feels towards the other; it feeds both the desire to 'succeed' and the terror of failure.

However great the release and potential power of this relationship for an actor, the sense of being 'locked into' the material he's performing, of being little more than an object on show, is never far away. The desperate need for 'feedback' is part of this, and if it seems vulgar or defensive to ask for it directly, actors have discovered a million subliminal methods to extract it from anyone in a position to supply it. Film and television have aggravated this situation still further. Not only do you get no immediate feedback in performance, but the acting techniques required are so different and have influenced audiences' expectations of acting so considerably, that the actor's sense of control over his own work and of the level and pitch of performance required of him is tenuous in the extreme.

At the same time, the whole world is fast becoming a globe of armchair critics. Slick production techniques and careful editing mean that the apparent standard of acting on TV is high, but put the same actors 'naked' on a live stage for two hours without the benefit of close-ups, cross-cutting and editing, and the huge disparity between the requirements of the two forms soon becomes apparent. As armchair critics, however, the differences in production are irrelevant to us. The only difference for an audience is that it has to travel to see a live performance and can't go for a pee during the commercials. The sense of 'separation' which exists thanks to the proscenium arch is therefore only enhanced by film and TV inasmuch as audiences have learnt to become more passive as consumers and yet also more critical. The very 'packaging' of our media renders their consumers more sophisticated critically yet less able to intervene on an active, political level about things they object to. The astonishing thing is that the same process has taken place amongst theatre practitioners watching each other's work. Placed in the same relationship as any audience to the material in hand, in spite of having the opportunity to intervene actively, the 'profession' still thrashes around in a welter of confused critical values when it comes to production.

This confusion is crucial to an understanding of how drama in the sixties was received and subsequently rebelled against. On the one hand drama was too 'flat', too banal: the emphasis on everyday realism in writing and acting which had been a great advance on the narrow artificiality of the drawing-room comedy and was so appropriate to the film and TV boom, seemed inadequate for the experience of live theatre. On the other hand, the very standards of social accuracy and awareness set by TV and film led people to feel uneasy about anything that was crudely 'theatrical'. In the attempt to synthesise these two quite polar opposites, vague terms like 'stylised' and 'heightened' abounded as people struggled to hit on the appropriate 'pitch' for live performance. As the classics came to be treated more soberly, and contemporary plays in 'heightened' ways, the term 'house style' became popular, suggesting a conscious and co-ordinated effort by companies to articulate a philosophical stance towards both old and new work. In nine cases out of ten such 'house styles' were little more than the resolution of the clash of cultural influences happening *outside* the theatre. In many cases they quickly degenerated into mannerisms, were soon recognised as such and superceded.

Part of the same malaise was the way in which class was treated. As opposed to the crude caricatures of Shaw, drawing-room comedy and British films of the forties, class had been introduced in a serious way through the accurate portrayal of working-class life in documentaries and TV 'kitchen sink' drama.This more 'democratic' realism carried over into the characterisations of playwrights like Pinter, Orton, Wesker and others. But it remained 'locked into' the surface reality which was the accepted emphasis of the time. Even Wesker and Arden, whose plays *did* explore class relations in some depth, became associated with the 'Angry Young Man' tag, which was principally the preserve of those who observed only the *trappings* of a peculiarly English version of class antagonism.

Even the colossal philosophical system of fail-safe devices represented by the work of Brecht failed to resist this porridge of intent and effect, medium and message, content and presentation. While his own plays were generally produced in every conceivable manner *except* a Brechtian one, any other play produced on a fairly sparse, open stage, accompanied by a narrator-figure or songs, received the (usually derogatory) epithet 'Brechtian'. His principal concept of 'alienation', that of seeing events on stage as something *un*-natural in order to sharpen an audience's awareness of the social and political motives behind them, was too much for the insular, chauvinist and anti-intellectual British tradition. The one existing philosophy of theatre which might have made some sense at least of the hodge-podge of class tension and anti-naturalistic preferences of the Establishment's opponents, was never consistently realised on the British stage. (At a conference on Brecht in Florence in 1973, while other countries spoke of their third and fourth editions of Brecht's collected works, John Willett had to declare apologetically that in England the first volume had only just come back from the printer.) So great was the confusion, it never seemed to occur to anyone that Brecht's arguments had been conducted largely within a proscenium-arch tradition, and that 'alienation' almost *depended* on its quality of 'separation'. Instead Brecht was embraced as ideal fodder for production in the proliferation of end-stage, in-the-round, octagonal, three-sided and 'environmental' auditoria which sprang up all over the country during the sixties' theatre boom. Consequently the rigour of Brecht's appeal to the conscious faculties of his audience was diluted and disappeared in a kind of osmosis between stage and auditorium.

Far greater than dissatisfaction with the proscenium arch was frustration at the inarticulacy and passivity of the sixties' 'living-room drama'. The very thought that all the skill and technique of the artists involved, their realism and wit all added up finally to something inexpressible seemed a denial of the purpose of theatre. The influence of documentary realism had placed such a premium on 'natural' dialogue, invariably employed in close, domestic, one-to-one situations where psychological consistency had to be scrupulously observed, meant that the facility to 'break out' from that was limited. Either a socking great symbol had to be introduced in best Ibsenite tradition to provide an overall image which made sense of the random and sometimes trivial goings-on of these characters with 'lives of their own', or there had to be a break in dramatic logic. There are two classic examples of this break in logic. The first is in Pinter's *Homecoming* where the dramatic tension of the first half of the play (and much of its best observation) is built on the *implicit* desire of the all-male family to 'possess' the woman. Once that desire has become explicit, however – in the simple stage direction 'LENNY *kisses* RUTH. *They stand, kissing.*' – that tension disappears, the characters' actions become ridiculous and the strengths of the play evaporate. Similarly in Stoppard's *Rosencrantz and Guildenstern*, after much deliberation (and the principal tension of the opening scene depending) on the exact nature of the relationship between imagination and reality, the coin comes down tails, the lights change and the two characters' 'context' – Shakespeare's original play – is supplied, completely sweeping aside their former rationale on stage, even to the extent of arch references to the audience. In both cases it is as if the very logical precision and tightness of the *writing*, of the dialogue to the situation it creates, in turn creates an impasse from which the author can only escape by a leap. The aesthetic and philosophical justification for *action* on stage was hard to find.

Demolishing the fourth wall

The kind of leap that fringe theatre workers of the seventies had in mind was entirely different. Instead of getting jammed in theatre conventions of one's own making, the desire was to explode the conventions. Instead of debating the nature of illusion and reality within the confines of the illusion of a theatre with its watchers and watched, the desire was to destroy the illusion. The plate-glass window in the frame of the proscenium arch shattered and the alarms began to sound. Actors stepped through the hole and began to talk directly to their audiences again – when, in fact, had they stopped? Not only that, but audiences were invited to step up and make the journey the other way. In *Hair* they were literally asked up on stage to dance at the end. It was the age of Pop Art and Happenings where real life was turned into an aesthetic event. Numerous productions were created with 'environmental' sets where the entire audience sat within the same decor as the actors, so that the division between acting and spectating areas was no longer clear. Almost every show found a device to involve the audience physically in the action of the play. 'Audience participation' became almost a necessary component of fringe productions, and auditoria noticeably filled up first from those seats furthest away from the likely acting area! My own fascination with these experiments ended one night in a Living Theatre production when two actors, fighting and scrambling their way up the gangway I sat adjacent to, accidentally elbowed me in the ear, sent my spectacles flying and dislodged a lens. (After that incident, I approached Peter Ansorge's excellent book on this era, *Disrupting the Spectacle*, with a certain, wry apprehension.)

These attempts at audience participation were of course crude and, like the stage vogue for nudity at the time, full-frontal. They did represent 'direct action' against traditional theatre's 'parcel game' and against its concomitant audience passivity, but most efforts were directed at the conventions of illusion while apparently relegating to second place the very advantage of theatre, that its illusions have something special to say. Saying that the conventions are wrong is not enough. The seemingly inexorable escalation of nudity and sex on stage to the point where people actually 'did it' (or tried to), demonstrated graphically the pointlessness of this pursuit. (Only ten years later in Howard Brenton's *Romans in Britain* did the actual act, in this case buggery, actually come to *mean* something.) Fun though it was, the sexual revolution on stage could go no further. And in hindsight the overall impact historically of these 'displays' of actual sexual relations was not very great. Economics, work, the family and the home have all remained stronger conditioners of sexual behaviour, as the revival of feminist thinking in the seventies has reminded us.

However, while aspects of sexual and women's liberation lend themselves readily to treatment within our existing theatre traditions because they can largely be expressed through individual and personal relations, the treatment of economic and class liberation depends much more on the depiction of mass movements in society. This implies not only different theatrical techniques, as Piscator discovered in the Berlin of the twenties, but also a different relationship to the audience. Instead of lobbing a revolutionary new thought or an emotional time-bomb into the network of relations surrounding our existing bourgeois culture (which is well able to absorb the shock), the need is for a new network, a new culture. Working at the Volksbühne, the 'theatre club' of the German Social Democratic Party, Piscator of course had this context ready provided,* but the political stirrings of the late sixties were directed independently of, and occasionally *against*, working-class organisation. In Britain in the late sixties, however direct and actual the shock tactics (including 'audience participation'), however much theatre conventions were attacked, audiences could not be robbed of their right to 'view' the performance. Dragging audiences physically into the action, confronting them with nude figures, stony silence or animals' entrails did not stop them 'keeping their distance'. Despising those audiences who reserved this right was not only implicitly undemocratic, it was unrealistic. Just as the state can legislate against certain kinds of art but not, finally, stop them being pursued, so artists can invite audiences to share but not *implicate* them in the value system behind a piece of theatre.

The response to this situation was that some theatre companies turned to new audiences out of distaste for the old ones. Others, more positively, looked to broaden or change the *class* composition of their 'constituency'. While some were trying to break out of conventional theatrical traditions towards, as it were, a more real world, others were engaged in actual political struggle and, seeing theatre as a direct and vivid means of communicating their point of view, were trying to break into the world of the imagination. In the wake of the new politics of the late sixties, the fact that theatre was in the flesh, that you were eyeball-to-eyeball with your audience and that a small troupe could go anywhere, do anything, was seen as a valuable means of political communication in the struggle against the increasingly 'corporate' politics of modern government, multinational capital, bureaucratic trades unions and the mass media. Whether at a demonstration, a tenants' meeting or as a factory-gate picket, the expression was direct, the stage was the real world and the audience were participating already! For many people, whether coming from theatre and encountering politics, or coming from politics and discovering theatre, the model of a simple action representing an aspect of contemporary life, played directly and simply not *to* an audience but *amongst* it, offered a potential for not only a new message but also a new method, one which wasn't corrupted by the 'parcel game' considerations of existing cultural traditions.

Enter the 'collective'

These traditions naturally included the hierarchical, hire-and fire system of theatre management, but also the idea of theatre director as mysterious conjuror, a Prospero who did or didn't renew your contract for reasons which remained obscure, and the idea of writer as gaoler, the man (usually) who kept everyone locked into his script. Once it was seen that there were other ways to make theatre, the lid came off the production system that until then had constrained its participants' temperaments. People rediscovered themselves as individual artists with their own motivations and perspectives towards both theatre and what it said about the world around them. Each individual connected with that world in a different way, and considerable pleasure accompanied the discovery of just how many different ways there were. Having thrown off the yoke of a single-minded, pyramidal system, no one was going

*See Erwin Piscator, *The Political Theatre*, Eyre Methuen, 1980.

to presume to impose their vision on anyone else. The common vehicle for expressing all these different viewpoints was the show itself. The form of organisation which was consequently adopted to devise the show was a 'co-operative' or 'collective' one.

There is a sense in which any theatre production is at the very least a collaborative effort. The initial idea and enthusiasm for a show, whether it comes from a director, an actor or from a written script, has to strike a chord in at least one other person on a level which, initially at least, is not circumscribed by a system of production. That sense of shared excitement can, in the best of worlds, be extended further to include the actors as a whole and, indeed, become the stimulus behind a whole production. It was this sense of artistic collaboration coming first – as opposed to the 'parcel game' where finance comes first – which lay at the root of the generation of most fringe productions in the seventies. It is no different from the enthusiasm with which a director and producer team up over an idea in the film industry or the West End theatre, except that a producing management as such is not, initially, involved. The further development of the show differs only in the same respect. Instead of a project being launched by raising private capital or managing public funds, shows on the Fringe were launched on labour power. Everyone involved in the project donated their time and energy to subsidise the work themselves, while the dole or part-time jobs subsidised their lives.

While this had the advantage of bringing everybody to the project on an equal basis, it had the disadvantage of falling prey to economic hierarchies outside the immediate work process. Men who were married with children, women who bore the responsibility for child-care, and anyone who had an aged parent, sick lover or a mortgage could not commit their time as whole-heartedly as others. Similarly, those who came from middle-class families with, if not the direct financial assistance of their parents then the security, contacts and plethora of hidden, material perks such a background brings, were more able to afford the luxury of these 'democratic' freedoms. Consequently it became a field of work in which there were more single, childless, middle-class, young men than any other sort of person. In this respect the difference from conventional theatre was not all that great.

Another distinguishing feature was that there were proportionately more actors – or aspirant actors – involved in these companies than any other skill. Whereas writers and directors can hope to get a reasonable amount of 'job satisfaction' out of the conventional system, and technicians whose position within the conventional hierarchy is comparable to that of actors, are often compensated by getting far better money, the 'collective' company offered actors a far greater liberation than anyone else. So, whereas in conventional theatre the number of administrative and technical staff would at least counterbalance the preponderance of actors as against director, writer and designer, the majority of 'company members' (for so they soon came to be called) in collective, fringe groups would invariably be actors.

The principle soon became established, however, that all company members should share in the necessary administrative and technical tasks. For many companies this principle extended to the point where there was no (declared) division of labour. Everyone was supposed to take on an equal number of tasks in every department. Naturally it often transpired that certain people took better to certain tasks than others, but 'artistic' rather than administrative or technical jobs remained the prize, and there was ample scope for backsliding. I remember on one production being up to my elbows in paint in a last-minute attempt to get a set decorated and looking up to see a company member who'd been heavily involved in administration wandering around casually like a foreman on a building site. I don't know to this day if this was because he felt he'd done enough 'boring' work or whether he just hated getting his hands dirty. Egalitarian principles did, however, mean that everyone had an equal interest (in both senses) in the work as a whole.

One aspect of that interest was quite new and, for many theatre workers, totally positive. The very motivation for working in theatre, the desire to express one's own experience of the world through the 'heightened' medium of an art form, could be satisfied directly, rather than by waiting to 'be asked'. Actors could choose or at least participate equally in the choice of the subject to be treated as they never can when they're simply hired to play a part. They were committed to the project from the word go, and this was a commitment which naturally showed in performance. In the late seventies an actor from Stratford, visiting a performance by Monstrous Regiment in the Midlands was struck forcibly by this quality and lamented the impossibility of an identical commitment from actors in the RSC. This is not to say that a comparable commitment cannot exist for actors in conventional theatre if the show and the work method are sympathetic; but the actors' control over these 'ifs' is slender. Commitment in the real sense is, ultimately, a matter of control, and the quality of involvement with a show's content still remains the most important and exciting aspect of the collective approach to producing theatre.

As time went on, however, other aspects of that 'interest' proved to be less positive. By taking on the *whole* of the problem – audiences, company organisation *and* the content of the shows – companies began inevitably to face some of the contradictions which had also been apparent in conventional semi-subsidised theatre. As ever, these contradictions had to do with the exercise of that new-found control, as much in relation to the forms of organisation and structure which supplanted the hire-and-fire system as with matters of aesthetic content and form.

6: COMMUNING WITH REVOLUTION

The idea of playing *amongst* an audience rather than *to* it is central to the idea of community theatre and remained very much a reality as long as the post-'68 groundswell of rebellion against the 'corporate' politics of the modern state continued. Even in the eighties, when the state is taking its revenge, the sense of a separate and distinct identity remains amongst companies who still adhere principally to a post-'68 value system. The groundswell has not increased but it has not noticeably diminished either. Some of the hope may have gone, but a generational coterie has survived the onslaught of the recession, retaining its own tastes and expectations and guaranteeing at least a modest audience for any show that celebrates its values. Since the Fringe was based on the sense of peripheral opposition to mainstream culture, it is well seasoned to withstand its present embattled situation. The great strength of the political Fringe – that its ideological opposition to the mainstream was so total – has meant that it still holds an attraction for anyone critical of the status quo. Its great weakness – that it attacked on all fronts simultaneously – means that it remains, very firmly, on the fringe.

Part of that total opposition, for socialist companies particularly, lay in the vision of a completely new social order. With the events of May 1968, the massive protests against the Vietnam war, the sit-ins of 1969 and 1970 and the miners' strikes of 1972 and 1974, the belief that revolution was just around the corner did not seem remarkable. Given that May 1968 failed, that the sit-ins produced only modest concessions and the miners settled for more money, the actual form that revolution might take was never clear. People did, however, have a sense of how it might *feel*. A sense of exhilaration, of camaraderie and release, a sense that in the nuclear age there might be a future worth the name – these feelings were shared both by theatre companies throwing off the yoke of hierarchical management and audiences escaping the dull conventionality of their jobs and traditional forms of entertainment. While it was possible in the here and now to celebrate together the breaks with tradition that had already happened, there was always a sense that these were just a prelude to something bigger and further-reaching.

The political Fringe offered a confirmation of these feelings. It was avant-garde in this respect, but it also tended to be vanguardist in its politics. It was 'other-worldly' in both the visionary and the absent-minded sense. That vision included a new kind of theatre which didn't yet exist. The values, methods and product of the Fringe were not going simply to co-exist with conventional theatre, they would replace them. This obviously depended on those bigger and further-reaching changes in society itself, but the exact timing of *those* remained a little obscure. For some, the answer to this lay in direct involvement in political activity itself. For others, involvement in the entertainment unions was what they knew and could tackle best. For others still, the very content of their work and the search for new audiences were themselves sufficient contribution to 'the struggle'. And there were indeed, both onstage and backstage, countless 'models' of a new order, where the visions of a radically transforming society were lived out in experimental form. Companies frequently worked on model collectivist lines; their plays strove towards the models of revolutionary drama. Paradoxically, the better these models were perfected within their own confines, the greater the illusion that they were influencing the bigger, realer world outside. Living in a commune, working in a collective which sought out working-class audiences and portraying a revolutionary heroine on stage *felt* right, but it didn't necessarily make the audience any bigger.

Community theatre, whether based in a venue or touring a locality, became in many ways the most self-contained of these illusory models. Whereas companies touring nationally bobbed like corks on a sea of fortune, labour movement 'gigs' came and went and arts-funding bodies' criteria changed from season to season, a show that played for a month in one place to full 100-seat houses of whom thirty to forty per cent were local, working-class people felt like a solid achievement. The roots had taken, the flower was in bloom, the plant would spread. The sneaking suspicion that the ground wasn't properly prepared was not exactly ignored; but given the huge problems in getting just that far, the temptation was, with one good production 'up', to rest on one's laurels. The theatre might be able to change the world, but the world had to put in a bit of effort too. After all, companies had their work cut out dealing with the encroachment of the world into their own operation.

Confronting the community

I indicated in Chapter Two some of the forms this encroachment takes in theatre as a whole, and community theatre is not exempt. Only the *forms* of encroachment were new. The fact that we all learn to develop our aesthetic sense from work we experience first as consumers meant that the legacy of unsuitable artistic models from the past had to be struggled against. The fact that any initiative within a capitalist system is subject from the beginning to the laws of the market-place made for difficulties in squaring the economic position of the company and its members with the content and method aspired to in its productions. The fact that these mini-businesses were springing up in a field where the anxieties, competitive urges and ambitions of the conventional production system were still dominant meant that defences had to be built against them. Anyone who imagines that because the small theatre companies of the seventies played to relatively small numbers of people and earned relatively small amounts of money, they were therefore composed of idle, feckless and witless incompetents, underestimates the size of the problem being tackled. Actually to take seriously the task of reaching the 'mass of the population' is a problem which successive waves of theatre practitioners have backed away from. If the efforts of these same small companies in the eighties seem less impressive than they once did, sheer exhaustion from moving mountains with only minimal help from the funding bodies and the cultural establishment is the cause.

The reality most fervently resisted was that any initiative within capitalism becomes subject to its laws. The books of Danny Cohn-Bendit were being *sold* (though quite a few were also being nicked). Most of the people working in fringe companies were young. They could postpone the realities of wages, rents, mortgages, child-care and career – for themselves and for a little while, at least. To live on the dole in a squat outside the mercantile, hierarchical values of the 'straight' world, simply to 'be', was an achievement in itself. For many it was also an extension of their education. When the problem of continuity arose, when it was no longer a question of the show which hit and ran, state funding from the Arts Council of Great Britain implied less of a compromise with the capitalist world than survival on the open market. Even so, I was astonished to find, in 1980, when trying to negotiate for the Theatre Writers Union a standard agreement for playwrights working with fringe companies, how many of these companies still could not, or would not, see themselves as managements. The desire not to be tarred with that particular brush, not to be implicated in any way in the running of an antipathetic system still prevailed – even though the people concerned were in fact holding and disbursing public funds.

The initial impetus of the Fringe had been *away from* existing institutions in both politics and theatre, towards the vision of its shows. That much was immediately possible. But to *continue* doing them, the Fringe depended on coming to terms with those institutions, on moving *towards* them, creating a network of relations for itself with audiences and the state which supplanted the relations of capitalist theatre. The artistic vision was 'other-wordly', but the social and administrative context in which it could continue had to be very much of this world. Whereas the vision of shows within conventional theatre can be totally radical (though it rarely is) yet continue to exist within that context, the radical vision of the Fringe implied a new context. No one rushed forward to supply that context, so companies had to work not only on their shows but also at the administrative tasks of raising audiences and grants.

The principal audience for the Fringe initially had been people from the same generation as the practitioners – the late sixties' generation of students and 'drop-outs' from both universities and 'straight' jobs. They read *Time Out* and frequented the arts labs, studio theatres, clubs, centres and students' unions which became the focus for anti-establishment culture. Companies which viewed their function more directly in the socialist perspective of reaching new working-class audiences soon became dissatisfied with this circuit and struck out towards establishing 'gigs' wherever working-class people might gather. This meant the street, outside factory gates, pubs and clubs, or performances for tenants, pensioners, local political parties and trade union meetings.

The very newness and differentness of performing theatre in these places presented its own problems. Not only would the show have to fit the venue physically (the set could never be too large), but it also had to fit in terms of its length in time and the suitability of its content and form. Jokes about leading trades unionists or the Labour Party which went down well in a student bar might receive a frostier treatment at a labour movement gig. Four-letter words or assumptions about sexual freedom might backfire on working-class men who'd brought their wives along. A play in which complicated arguments were presented through long, realistic scenes was wholly inappropriate for audiences with pints in their hands waiting for the juggler to come on.

The very act of taking a new content to a new audience meant that new forms had to be found. Building a more permanent relationship with audiences depended on whether the *whole* of the experience presented was something that audience might want again. For touring companies the sheer physical problems of getting the set in, making sure there was sufficient electrical power and adequate seating – not to mention publicity – often created friction between the company's administration and the 'contact' at the gig. Conversely, the very sight of people engaged in hard, physical labour before becoming 'an actor' sometimes endeared the troupe to its audience in itself. When the all-female Womens Theatre Group appeared and did the same without the assistance of a single man, a further point was made. For venues, the quality of the building and seats, the state of the foyer and the provision of food and drink became more crucial than the show. This problem dogged the Half Moon regularly for the first ten years of its life. The shows were still a largely unknown quantity, and so persuading local authorities, local arts bodies, local councillors, trades unionists and campaigners for tenants, pensioners, ethnic minorities and the women's movement that the work was *not* amateur, that it was not just political propaganda, that their audiences *would* enjoy it but that it needed a lot of publicity became a full-time occupation in itself.

Companies recognised this and began to acquire people specifically designated as administrators. This breach of the (often unwritten) 'no-division-of-labour' principle carried its own problems. Unless the administrator knew the company's work intimately, knew the audience contacts well and had the right manner, liaison between the companies and the gig could turn sour. If a show was described one way and turned out another it could create bad feeling. Actors might blame the administrator, but the administrator could equally well blame the company for not briefing him or her properly. After lengthy protestations that the company were all socialists committed to playing to working-class audiences, the sight after the show of an exhausted acting company huddled together for comfort at one end of the bar ignoring their audience with seeming aloofness stretched the credibility of more than one hard-working local contact. The occasional drunken brawl, political slanging-match or clash of accents between social classes could destroy in minutes a relationship built through months of patient work. The sheer difference in life-style (people breezing in and out, not too concerned about punctuality, the tendency to side-step formality and address everyone familiarly) often made for abrasive confrontations between the two ends of the operation.

Occasionally a fringe company's visit would prove entirely successful, whereupon the sheer joy of discovering that the potential everyone hoped for actually existed and could be built on, would give a transitory illusion of total success. It would then transpire that the company could not return for another six months, and that when they did there was a completely different, and much less efficient organiser, and a completely different audience. Many theatre-in-education companies encountered this problem early on and restricted their circuits in order to build up a regular relationship with their schools' audiences. For venues, the difficulty of ensuring that *every* show had *all* the right ingredients (and the venues couldn't make one show last for several months), sometimes proved insurmountable. Even if the shows were roughly on the right lines, problems with the seating or the lighting or the involvement of local people might make for audience disapproval. As the 'hidden demand' was discovered (rather like that for teeth 'n' specs when the National Health schemes were introduced), companies might not find themselves flexible or adaptable enough to respond to the requirements the community itself began to voice. As the problems were uncovered and the successes built on, the need for greater subsidy became obvious. The only way to overcome the problems thrown up by this entirely new set of relationships was to employ more people, give them more time to grapple with the problems and have the arts bodies actively engaged in the process. By the time these discoveries were being made however, the oil crisis of 1973 was beginning to bite, Denis Healey was talking to the IMF, and the boom days of arts subsidy were already numbered. From now on growth in this area would be much, much harder. The experiment was nipped in the bud.

The perils of Piccadilly

From the beginning, the obvious place to go to for grants was the Arts Council of Great Britain. Generally more forward-looking than local bodies, the ACGB was not slow – by its own standards – to respond to the new developments of the Fringe. But anyone who imagines that the socialisation of our culture can be achieved simply by setting up a state arts body to administer funds to the 'right' applicants underestimates the complexity of the issues involved. Every regional theatre, as previously described, has a board to preside over the spending of its public money. The fringe companies had no equivalent 'responsible' body. They had taken responsibility for the nation's culture into their own hands. The socialist companies felt furthermore that they were returning culture to the 95 per cent of the population who paid for it but didn't get it. They had an automatic right to the money. The Arts Council, lacking criteria other than their 'professional advisers', saw things somewhat differently. They 'responded' (all that, by their charter, they are entitled to do) to the new initiatives of the Fringe by supplying grants for individual projects by people whose work was already in some way proven, and, as some companies grew and stabilised, by supplying revenue grants for year-long programmes of productions; but since these companies had no boards, no recognised managements as such, they dealt with companies directly and their function as 'watchdog' increased. After all, the ACGB itself is watched closely by the Right and has constantly to be able to demonstrate the social benefit of its activities.

Inevitably, as the Fringe grew and companies like 7:84, Belt and Braces, Red Ladder, the Half Moon and the Albany demonstrated that their work was artistically sound, the demand for more subsidy meant that the ACGB's need to demonstrate that it was dealing with responsible parties also grew. It began to require that companies constitute themselves formally and in this way imposed the very status of management on companies which many were reluctant to accept. Particularly for those companies influenced by anarchist or libertarian thinking, this came to seem like the state imposing its own values on its detractors, rendering them harmless (because answerable to 'above') and introducing a certain measure of political control.

There is no doubt that in the wake of increased and renewed ACGB funding many companies began to 'tone down' their work. But this was not exclusively the consequence of management status being imposed. Certainly, some companies would explicitly consider the likely response of the ACGB at the year's end to their programme of work, but many were determined to take the money *and* continue to say what they wanted to the audience they wanted. For some, no doubt, the 'respectability' of an ACGB grant acted as a subliminal censor and, compounded with weariness at conducting an uphill struggle, made a 'softer' line seem the easier option.

Many companies were already beginning to develop their policies in more complex ways. The simple, bald, exclamatory form of much early agit-prop, observed to be no longer sufficiently persuasive, was being superceded. Yet other companies found that their audiences, with whom they now held at least the beginnings of a firm and regular relationship, were feeding in *their* experience, challenging assumptions and demanding an approach which took *their* reality into account. Newspaper reviews mattered much less than in conventional theatre. They might help when sending out publicity for a tour, but a group's reputation was usually a more significant factor. Venues like the Half Moon depended on them more, but the Albany had made a sufficient mark on its local community not to worry too desperately.

Throughout the late seventies the Arts Council strenuously denied that it acted in any way as a political censor. When challenged, it would always point to 'standards' (a dubious criterion in contemporary theatre, for the reasons proposed at the end of Chapter Three). Consequently it refused or cut grants to the poorer, less illustrious companies who did not attract the most gifted actors and who, by going into the toughest areas to find their audience, could not point to high box-office takings. It took an attack from Sally Oppenheim on an *Any Questions* programme in January 1983 to elicit from Sir Roy Shaw (after he'd left the Arts Council) the admission that if companies' work seemed too much like socialist propaganda, they got their grants cut.

Actors' power

Not only did the status of management (doing the state's dirty work for it) sit uneasily on the shoulders of many socialist acting companies, it also compounded certain difficulties posed by continuity itself. The Fringe's initial emphasis on labour power was experienced as a revolution, a liberation from hierarchy, a turning upside down of traditional functions in theatre production; and because of the increasing consciousness among many actors of themselves as the 'workers' in theatre, that labour power quickly became associated with 'actors' power'. (It was also the age of Black Power and Flower Power.) Out with the bathwater of creativity-stifling management, however, also went – initially at least – the baby of writing and directorial skills. Writers and directors tended to be viewed not as collaborators in the artistic sense but, because of their traditional position in the conventional theatre hierarchy, as collaborators with management. Actors, it was felt, could do without them in the drive towards a new kind of expression which got away from the literary, verbal, schematised, naturalistic, over-intellectual and fundamentally *unpopular* theatre of the sixties. In spite of the fact that writers and directors were actually working alongside them on absolutely the same basis, likewise donating their labour, and in spite of many of them voluntarily dismantling their traditional privileges, mistrust remained. In many cases the drive to untrammelled actors' self-expression was absolute.

For some this drive was totally unconnected with the question of audience. For others the desire to establish a new audience relationship was essential, but writing and directing were seen as functions which obstructed that relationship. The emphasis was on the here and now, the immediate effect, the moment of contact with the audience in performance which only actors experience. All other considerations were looked on as a smokescreen to protect writers' or directors' interests, or as a hang-over from the old, compromised system, and so dismissed. In a spirit of experiment (and sometimes of sheer funk), many writers and directors went along with this. Directors could back off so far under the weight of actors' pressure that scripts could be torn apart or completely misrepresented. Writers could side with actors' wishes against the director's and effectively undermine his authority and the unity of the production. In the best situations people re-learned their skills in a reciprocal give-and-take with the others. But the myth that actors are at the only 'sharp end' of the business was gradually destroyed as acting companies struggled with the devising of scripts, the unification of production style, the organisation of tours and publicity and all the other tasks which, traditionally, they are spared. As companies saw the value of 'taking on' writers, directors and designers for individual shows, this dictatorship of the theatrical proletariat negotiated a series of new understandings about responsibilities with each respective skill. Those of us who survived the Terror believe these are a vast improvement on the atrophied power structure of conventional theatre.

Other pressures also modified the 'collective' principle. The rigours of touring in a nine-seater van, working in dressing-rooms the size of cupboards, and surviving on small grants or the dole, coupled with working through fundamental questions about the content of plays and matters of organisation, meant that people could not always afford – financially, physically or emotionally – to work with companies for very long. Changes in personnel occurred and, with the onset of subsidy, some companies expanded. The democratic principle of everyone's labour power being equal was complicated by the fact that the labour power had now congealed as capital. The group's grant and equipment had been *earned* by the original company members. They might not worry about that so much, but the agreed principles on which the company had been set up would inevitably be subject to the pressure for change as the times, the group's operations and its personnel changed. New members might view the company's former operations critically; they might, initially at least, see themselves as being taken on in the sense of employed, rather than simply 'joining'; old members might worry that the group's identity could become blurred.

These changes put perhaps more strain than any other consideration on the 'everyone-is-equal-no-division-of-labour' principle of collective companies. Surely there had to be *some* mechanism whereby the hard effort of original company members was given emphasis within the company's operation, even if only as protection against the fly-by-night new member who joins, turns out not to give a fig for the founding principles and wants to take the company off in a completely new direction. Other difficulties could exacerbate this situation still further.

Peer-group pressure

In any theatre company the difficulty of having to do a job of work in a very few weeks with people you may not have met before is alleviated by a set of habits and customs implying a value-system within which people feel secure. Within a few days, during discussions in the pub at lunch-time, by having a quick moan about the money and the director (but at the same time re-assuring others that one is not going to cause trouble), by indicating reservations about the plays one's performing (but again re-assuring the others that one will not give less than full commitment), a sense of togetherness is established which overcomes run-of-the-mill problems in rehearsal. By this means a kind of peer-group pressure is established amongst the majority of the company, from which only the bumptious, the over-intellectual, the exceptionally talented, untalented or withdrawn are excluded. The customary attitude towards such outsiders, however, is extremely tolerant. Typically British politeness and middle-class 'breeding' ensure that there is rarely a direct confrontation with such 'outsiders'. Sometimes a few gentle hints may be dropped, sometimes an unacknowledged leader of the peer-group may be detailed to 'have a talk' with the outsider, but although there is invariably at least one person outside this cosy consensus, it is extremely rare that antagonism comes out into the open. The sense of 'pulling together' is too important to everyone. Jobs are too scarce and the money too poor for anyone to be further victimised. It is very rare indeed in British theatre for an actor to be sacked in mid-rehearsal. Once the show is up and the contracts expire however, it is a different matter. Since there will be an inevitable re-shuffling for the next season and since some will leave of their own accord anyway, this is the time when subterranean tensions surface and influence who will stay with the company.

Since collective companies have no officially acknowledged management however, the cosy solidarity which lasts for one production, during which such 'personnel' problems can be off-loaded on to management, is rendered more problematic. Based on labour-power, with no employer, the assumption amongst collective companies is that, unless otherwise stated, a company member is with the company for good – or at least until he or she wishes to leave.

But peer-group pressure remains, and on the Fringe it is not just a question of muddling through together as actors but also of devising whole shows together. Questions of ideas and belief enter into play as well as those of personality, and are further complicated by the company *as a whole* having responsibility for its own organisation. In these circumstances, coping with an 'outsider' is many, many more times difficult. The question cannot necessarily be shelved until after the show is on, as it might seriously influence the show's content or style away from the group's usual output. But when it is raised, it will necessarily involve a long discussion about everything the group stands for, from top to bottom, with each item given varying and sometimes contradictory emphasis from each group member. It may even finally involve a sacking which no one wants to admit responsibility for. What then happens is that the acting company's traditional method of hints and 'talkings-to' grows in intensity. If the hints aren't taken, or are misunderstood, or if the outsider in question, however willing, seems incapable of change, the intensity of this pressure can become very unpleasant. The worst part of being sacked, after all, is not so much stopping work as not being wanted. Hearing a million ways in which you're not wanted before you're finally told to 'go away' can be very painful indeed.

Anthropologists might suggest that any group in society needs a leader of some sort and a scapegoat in order to confirm its own identity. In the age of Thatcher and four million unemployed, it might be more sensible to recognise that any group attempting to cohere around a practical task in its collective interest will find some of its members more suited to it than others. The answer must surely lie in a formal mechanism whereby power and authority are openly declared, where responsibility can be admitted on both sides, and where the break, if it comes, can be made cleanly and without emotional blackmail.

In the early days of the Fringe when everyone came fresh to the work, convinced that the Show to End All Shows was just around the corner, conflicting attitudes on anything from the script to the colour of the poster could well end in a head-on, blazing row. In some ways this was healthier than the kind of nagging, long-term antagonisms which can grow up if a company sustains its activities over a longer period. Everyone, after all, is subject to slightly different aesthetic and social conditioning which will make the emphasis of their individual creative input different. The moment the Fringe got beyond the simple, broad truths which needed stating because they weren't being stated elsewhere, these problems of individual vision began to arise. As companies recognised the necessity for taking on writers, directors and designers, the customary 'overall' view which is part of these skills sometimes conflicted with the 'overall' view of the group. In this way these specialists could become outsiders by virtue of their function rather than their attitude. Artistic consistency became confused with organisational control.

Some hardened cynics would point to these confusions and observe that amongst any group of people a struggle for power is inevitable and that one person will emerge from it as victor; others would mutter wisely that all artistic enterprises were inevitably, and best, dominated by one individual; those who remained committed to the collective approach might listen to these comments and see them as an apology by their proponents for their own quiescence. The loss of creative potential which autocracy frequently generates was a problem such apologists had no answer for.

Aesthetic development and Arts Council requirements were making the problem of managerial responsibility more acute. And whereas an individual autocrat can act blindly, collective autocracy requires a self-conscious decision. Actors are used to being guiltless in such matters – on the side of the angels. As a consequence, many acting companies failed both to seize the opportunity that was offered and to face up to its responsibilities. Much of the Fringe's work at this time fell more within the declared remit of the Arts Council than the second-class sub-commercial theatre it was mainly subsidising. Had companies been more generally willing to 'get their hands dirty' and openly exert their collective managerial authority in a positive way, its surreptitious and negative operation might not have impeded the full development of individual skills and vision to the groups' overall aims.

Some companies did respond to these problems by turning to a two-tier structure whereby, after a period of recognised service, a 'new' member could be admitted to an inner circle of founding or long-term members. This defensive measure was often experienced as aggression by actors and freelancers taken on by these companies. They could often come to feel attacked by principles founded on past experience of which they had no direct knowledge; and since the principles extended from the content of shows through the organisation of the company to its relationship with audiences, an attack on any one of these fronts could be received as being on all of them. 'Not only are you a bad actor/writer/director but your manner is too bourgeois, you disrupt the company and have no right to call yourself a socialist.' Not having your contract renewed in conventional theatre was a benison by comparison.

7:THE WHAT? MUST GO ON

Whatever else their audiences might have expected from these companies, at the very least it expected a show. Not turning up because the van broke down, because a company member was ill or the show not ready, was the worst thing that could happen. Performance is after all the point of contact with the audience, the forum in which the active dialogue between practitioners and consumers takes place. Self-evident though this is, it is not the most important ingredient in the total picture. Whatever the show, it is firstly the relations of production within the company then of practitioners to their material and only finally of practitioners to the audience itself which ultimately govern the outcome. When the Half Moon's production of Brecht's *The Mother* tranferred to the Round House, for example, although the production and personnel were identical, the particular experience the show offered was vastly altered by the move to a bigger building, with a different producing management and an NW3 audience rather than the usual pilgrims to E1. Where control over these relations is beyond one's power, however, the show is most certainly the thing; and given that for companies in the seventies, questions of a show's audience and environment were as important as its content and style, the struggles to 'get it right' were considerable.

It is impossible here to catalogue the many different approaches to shows adopted by what amounts to more than 200 companies over fifteen years but, naturally enough, if you decide to do away with the legacy of your own cultural tradition, you have to start right from scratch. As any full-time writer faced daily with the Terror of the Blank Page will testify, to do so takes not just courage but a certain foolhardiness. In some cases, therefore, in order to overcome this Terror, either a director with the company or directorial instincts within certain company members might propose a 'concept': perhaps a direct adaptation of an existing play, perhaps a story from history or fiction suitable for dramatisation, or simply an image (implying a situation or a setting). But given that many companies approached their theatre in the first place from a *political* involvement, the work process frequently began by taking a current *issue*, which meant that every company member could contribute to the treatment of that issue on an equal basis.

The very open-endedness of issues, their advantage as a starting-point, brought with it, however, the disadvantage of finding a cohesive angle from which to approach them. Massive subjects like unemployment, The British in Ireland, Equal Rights and so on need the key of a story, a central image, or at the very least an *approach* to unlock them. Necessarily, however, any such key proposed by an individual company member starts off as a subjective angle on an objective dilemma. Imaginative responses to the world's problems rarely come divisible from the experience, energy and skill of the individual who dreams them up. It is very hard to have a collective fantasy. If one particular aspect of a suggested aesthetic approach displeased another company member, the whole idea could fall. To attempt to qualify another's idea could be extremely dangerous in that it might impair the dramatic wholeness or dynamic of the original suggestion. The best collectively devised shows of this kind were those like the Women's Theatre Group's *My Mother Said* (about sex education) where there was a shared base of *experience* as well as a common consciousness about the subject in hand. The fleshing out of analysis, either in terms of characterisation or theatrical presentation, was all-important, whether the starting-point was real life or other dramatic work. This was particularly important to the actors themselves, as it was they who would eventually be realising the material. Paradoxically, however, actors were frequently so concerned to exercise their newly-won control over the overall 'line', they left themselves little room to develop their actual acting. The over-riding importance of finding a *story* to express the play's concerns through the dynamic of a dramatic action (thus providing something to actually *act*) was frequently ignored./

Another important lesson, rarely learnt, was the difference between the playscript as what I shall call here 'output' and 'intake'. Acting companies in the seventies were keen to *express* their own ideas and frequently felt that the best way they could control the material was by working it up through improvisation. I worked as 'typewriter' for such exercises on two or three occasions – a process whereby either the company themselves or a writer and director work from a general synopsis and set up a series of short scenarios for the actors to improvise. In this situation the writer sits in on the impros or workshops, takes notes and 'writes up' the ensuing scenes after rehearsal – a process involving the writer, incidentally, in considerable overtime. As most playwrights know, however, their 'output' has to be carefully crafted if the way it's to be 'taken in' by actors before it's eventually 'put out' again for an audience is to achieve the desired effect. After it's written up in this way the resulting scene is usually read through by the company. On one occasion when I was in this situation the actors complained every day that what I'd written up the night before did not properly reflect what they'd done the previous day. Exasperated by this, I eventually brought a tape-recorder into rehearsal and typed up that day's impros verbatim (a much easier, though soulless task) before presenting them the following morning. The response was still: 'This isn't what we did yesterday' – and of course the response was correct. The 'intake' of reading from a script can never *feel* like the 'output' of improvisation, and only by working on how you rediscover the dynamic and excitement behind the original work (a process which in conventional theatre is called rehearsal!) can you make 'intake' and 'output' identical. Even then, the very excitement of improvisation lies in not knowing how things may turn out. Frequently when you *do* know, they become much less exciting. The criteria of improvised and scripted drama are of course quite different. The trick – which is the job I had been attempting to work at – is to integrate the most exciting discoveries of the impros into a text which, in deliberate form, can best express the best aspects of the company's collective 'output' for an audience.

Even if the eventual product from this and similar processes fitted the acting company perfectly, there was no guarantee it would work as a text in its own right and consequently be usable by another company. This became more important later on when companies were better established, had learned about the difficulties and time consumed in devising their own shows, and looked around for plays by like-minded companies which might suit their own requirements.

Writers and directors working with collective acting companies and perhaps more accustomed to arriving at and thinking through the dramatic 'key' to an issue, might often find themselves making suggestions which were then 'qualified' out of viability. Passing the buck of the blank page to a writer or director, actors would sometimes chip in with their requirements as if giving a shopping-list to an errand-boy. Everyone had The Big One, the Play to End All Plays in mind, but everyone's perfect play was different. Being open to suggestion often meant taking quite contradictory suggestions on board. The mistake was made of handing responsibility back to writers and directors but wanting simultaneously to retain control. Rarely were 'outsiders', including designers, given a genuine collective brief; more likely was a hotch-potch of demands. The more 'democratically' the outsider tried to satisty *all* demands, the more likely the result would please no one. This lack of responsibility towards outsiders had a further, organisational spin-off. In (often lengthy) discussion of a democratic basis for wages and conditions, it was only recognised very late in the day that self-employed writers, directors and designers receive no sick or holiday pay and often don't qualify for dole.

'-Isms' revisited

These difficulties were compounded further. For many companies, getting the 'right line' on a show's subject-matter, being politically 'correct', became a major consideration. Since they were founded in opposition to traditional forms of theatre, this pursuit of political consistency was understandable. There was no point in simply repeating the mistakes of the past. It meant, however, that ideas in the show had to be thought through from top to bottom – not only in reference to its politics but also considering the effect of certain aesthetic approaches on audiences' perception of that subject-matter.

Perhaps the principal example of this was the problem of 'realism' or 'naturalism' – terms often used indiscriminately and without much agreed definition. Conventional theatre in Britain has a tradition of 'realism' from Shakespeare to Osborne, but for companies attempting to change their audiences' perception of the world, the simple reflection (even refraction) of life as it is lived posed considerable problems. We know for example from advertisements that the apparently straightforward reproduction of 'meaningful' slices of life are no such thing. Whether sipping Martini on riviera beaches, smoking Stuyvesant in helicopters, drinking John Bull in Romford or settling down snugly in front of a British Gas fire, every slice is idealised. In the process of idealisation certain existing values are reproduced and magnified. Every cloth-cap worker reproduces The Cloth-Cap Worker, every football hooligan The Football Hooligan, every dolly bird The Dolly Bird, and so on.

It's difficult, however to mount a critique of reality without showing that reality. Show it in the wrong way, and you simply confirm it. I remember seeing several shows ostensibly attacking the idea of women as sex objects which, in order to make their point, presented the actresses in fishnet tights and low-cut tops – thus scoring, for many of its audience, an own goal. The platitude that satirists at some level love the target of their attacks found a new meaning for companies struggling to 'show' without appearing to confirm. Many of them eschewed the work of their contemporary 'political' playwrights for the same reasons. The tendency towards an 'imagistic' approach in the work of playwrights like Howard Brenton and Snoo Wilson had the advantage of representing a social *argument* on stage but appeared to approach the characters from the outside, demonstrating scant knowledge or analysis of their *actual* situation. On the other hand the fictions of more realistic playwrights like David Hare and Trevor Griffiths, who did get 'into' their characters, seemed to represent a more finite, immutable reality. When all conventions are up for grabs, the playwright can't win either way. No surprise then that the number of successful and sustained collaborations between playwrights and fringe companies over the past fifteen years has remained very small indeed; but criticism of their contemporary playwrights' product and, occasionally, fear of the unknown consequences of collaboration did not overcome the Terror of the Blank Page.

Unlike the semi-subsidised regional reps, however, companies did not fall back on the easy option of producing the tried and tested classics (the Supermarket's Best Buys). All too often classics are produced not because of any startlingly original re-interpretation but because of a company's need to balance the books or a director's need to develop a 'profile'. After all, the easiest yardstick by which to judge directors' talent is to compare their productions of *Hamlet*. But the refusal to fall back on the classics does finally speak of a desire to rediscover the value of theatre in a way with which only the most radical and consistent re-interpretations of the classics can compete. (A joint attack in 1981 by national newspaper reviewers Michael Billington and Michael Coveney on the Fringe and its directors for ignoring the classics finally broke the close identification of at least four young directors with new work, since when several productions have trod the well-worn paths of the sixties. Practitioners always protest the contrary, but this demonstrates the direct effect on 'profile'-consciousness of even the most uninformed and backward-looking comment. While it is certainly true that there is not enough good new work to sustain dozens of companies all year round, the abandonment of the pursuit of new work invariably represents the triumph of the pressures of 'the business' over a director or a company's creative originality. The difficulties fringe companies faced were not therefore due to a lack of *critical* awareness but to a levelling-off of creative originality no more acute than in conventional theatre. Companies knew what they didn't want, but in struggling to find what they did want, a collective view of the present was more useful to them than an individual view from either present or past.

These collective aesthetic principles began to harden at the same time as embryonic managements formed around companies' originating members and their principles of organisation. Since both the shows and their structure of organisation expressed the company's collective view, it was very easy to confuse the two, especially where actors were seen as 'the workers' in theatre. Many companies began to feel that their formula for a socialist or more liberated theatre was the only 'correct' one, and that by retaining power on 'correct' principles on the workers' behalf they were acting in the best Leninist tradition. 'Right-onism' was born in both company organisation and the content of productions.

Its consequences in one of these aspects of a company's work could have unfortunate effects in the other. One company I was commissioned to write for held workshops on our project together before its summer break – a practical way for actors to have an input and a measure of control within a group effort where the writer is subsequently to go away and write alone. At the end of the workshops the director, with whom both I and the company had enjoyed working, left the project because he saw a contradiction in this question of 'control' between the group of six actors who were making their requirements of the project known, and the 'upper tier' of the company's ultimate management. As a result of organisational tensions within the company arising from their previous tour, four out of the six actors left the company in the course of the summer, during which I was writing a script designed to fit them, as performers, like a glove. When the script was completed and came to be re-cast, actors were chosen as much, if not more, on the basis of their suitability as 'company members' – aspects of political and trade union consciousness, familiarity with collective companies, etc., – as on their suitability for the parts. One of the two remaining actors consequently switched parts, and a play which had originally been intended specially to fit its performers ended up with only one of its original instigators *in situ*. The show was a shambles and eventually taken off, and the 'politically suitable' company members sacked because of their artistic *un*suitability.

Companies didn't have to call themselves socialist to operate in this way, but for some of those who did, the heat of an imminently expected revolutionary dawn led them to associate the release of 'actors' power' with the throwing off of other forms of social oppression.

The influence of the Workers Revolutionary Party has become associated in many people's minds with some of these attitudes, possibly because of their considerable influence at this time as self-proclaimed leaders of the Left within the actors' union, Equity. But within many companies the influence of the Socialist Workers Party, the International Marxist Group and various Maoist organisations was comparably strong, and none of these organisations, to my knowledge, based their vision of a socialist future on the principle of actors' power. The fact was that people felt an urgent need to contribute politically, that theatre offered a means of communicating new political ideas directly, and that the structures of the old production system were too strongly identified with the old ideas. Part of this approach was justified. Even the best of the British theatre tradition with its emphasis on realism – reflecting a traditional political emphasis on pragmatism – is chronically suspicious of ideas. And many of the structures, habits and beliefs of the 'parcel game' system provide a cast-iron insurance against pressure from 'below'. But as important a factor in the identification of actor with 'worker' was guilt. Important political questions had to be addressed, yes, but addressing them in the theatre was easier than addressing them in politics itself. Whether people came from working-class backgrounds and felt guilt towards their origins, or from middle-class backgrounds and felt guilt about what they'd never known, the sense of compensating for moral unease so brilliantly characterised by Lenin as 'an infantile disorder' was rampant. It led in many cases to a 'leftier-than-thou' attitude where the criterion was to be up-to-the- minute with the latest far-left critiques – often of 'old' Left positions – through which the forces of reaction were imminently expected to drive a coach-and-four.

This emphasis on political analysis and discussion did, however, tend to favour the most articulate and politically educated. These were often the people who had more experience of directing and writing. At the same time it tended to militate against the 'inspirational' actor who, uncluttered with intellectual baggage, might well get straight to the actual point in performance. It also militated against people who had more direct experience of the conditions of working-class life but less book-learning. People in both categories might feel unease at the intellectuals' 'right-line-ism', but if they dared to voice an objection, they might well find themselves out-argued. This in turn fostered an anti-intellectualism not far removed from the resentment of Oxbridge old-boy dominance which is rife (and not entirely unjustified) in the subsidised sector. In some ways the divisions of conventional theatre were coming to be reproduced even within this supposedly egalitarian system. However strong the British anti-intellectual tradition, those who felt insecure in their political education found themselves looking over their shoulder, afraid to speak for fear the company guru (and there was usually at least one, fresh from the mountain, carrying the tablets of Marx, Lenin, Trotsky, Mao, Althusser or Lacan) would jump down their throats. Once again it seemed to be the university-educated, middle class who led and those with the most direct and immediate experience who followed. Not only actors from working-class backgrounds but also certain women, gays and black people felt that their *experience* of oppression was being glibly packaged not in the commercial 'parcel game' but in terms of political dominance.

Some companies split under this pressure, and increasing consciousness of these dichotomies coincided with the gathering strength of the women's movement in the mid-seventies to give many women the self-confidence to form their own groups. The faculty of *listening* to each other and of acting collectively – faculties encouraged by the women's movement – soon made these groups' operation more satisfactory for their members. The suitability of 'personal' politics to dramatic treatment made them artistically satisfying as well; but in the meantime some of the moral imperatives and critiques of feminist consciousness have come to be exerted in a manner similar to the 'leftier-than-thou' attitudes of the self-styled Leninists, thus establishing a new sexism. For some, the prospect of the socialist-feminist Fringe tearing itself apart on the myriad guilt-trips of gender, class and race is a sad development of its original anti-Establishment solidarity.

Mingled with these anxieties, however, were the sheer exhilaration of confronting new ideas, the joy of devising new techniques to express them, and the pleasure of discovering a lost world behind the façades of our dominant culture. People were angry that Marx, Owen, William Morris and the feminist classics had been conspicuously absent from their university syllabuses. The whole history of socialist and feminist culture was discovered to have been suppressed. Even within the field of drama no real documentation of the Workers Theatre Movement, of Unity Theatre, Joan Littlewood, Wesker's Centre 42 and other working-class or socialist initiatives existed. It is only recently – and just in time – that Raphael Samuel's excellent work with Ruskin College's History Workshop* has unearthed much valuable material. As a consequence people have had to learn by trial-and-error, making mistakes as they went along, instead of being able to refer to accounts of similar initiatives in the previous decades where similar problems had been encountered and similar mistakes made.

It was also possible, however, with the best democratic will in the world, for so many different and sometimes quite contradictory viewpoints to be brought to bear on the 'issue' at hand that the inspiration of the original idea was lost under the weight of everyone chipping in. The need to listen to everyone, to examine the issue from every conceivable point of view tended to destroy the unifying vision which is so important for an audience whose first need is to orient themselves within the scope of what's being presented. This 'get-it-all-in-ism' led to some incredibly rambling, shapeless shows, but from time to time the very rawness of the experience described, or the very originality of subject-matter and treatment, made the consequent productions real eye-openers to the growing band of followers they were attracting.

Some rise, some fall

With the success of plays like Belt and Braces' *Weight* and *Mrs Collypepper*, Monstrous Regiment's *Scum* and *Vinegar Tom*, the Women's Theatre Group's *My Mother Says* and *On The Costa Del Trico*, Red Ladder's *Strike While the Iron is Hot* and *Taking Our Time*, Gay Sweatshop's *Care and Control* and *Dear Love of Comrades*, John McGrath's plays for 7:84, my own for the Half Moon and John

*See particularly *History Workshop, 4* (Autumn 1977).

Turner's for the Combination at the Albany, political fringe theatre through the seventies had established a relationship with its audience which was entirely new. Based on a broadly common political understanding as well as common aesthetic expectations, the division between product and consumer was replaced by the bond of interest between practitioners and spectators. Differences of emphasis in content remained, as did differences in methods of organisation, but the sense of a 'movement' remained intact. Even the parameters of an aesthetic consensus emerged, based on a realism which took seriously the predicaments of its characters' lives yet also attempted to relate these to broader social or historical events and a political analysis of them. The courageous (and sometimes reckless) publication of these plays, principally by Journeyman Press and Pluto Press, contributed to the sense of a milestone being reached. To the next generation of theatre workers leaving the schools and colleges, these plays were already 'established' in the sense that they were conditioning taste and were there to be rebelled against.

But however willing companies were to develop in the light of experience and criticism, the effects of the recession through the late seventies meant that their work could not grow – either in scale or in the demonstration of mature expertise. Grants did not keep pace with inflation, so companies remained the same size and could not afford to increase production costs. At the same time the number of paid jobs in all aspects of the industry remained static or decreased, leading on the one hand to increasing conservatism, on the other hand to a 'new Fringe'. In the scramble for the few remaining life-rafts that existed, several principles – and more than a few bodies – were thrown overboard. Artistic directors pulled in their horns and did fewer new plays. While the younger generation of reviewers eyed the 'top jobs' on national newspapers and established their right-wing credentials, the established reviewers drew up the ladders and developed a harsher tone. Individuals in all branches of the business who'd felt, or been made to feel, uncomfortable during the heyday of far-left politics crept out of the woodwork and took their revenge. By the time Margaret Thatcher became Prime Minister, the cultural climate in Britain had already blown with the rightward wind. How much of a coincidence was it that the home-bases of Red Ladder, Unity Theatre, the Albany and the Half Moon all suffered from vandalism and fires, probably inflicted by extreme right-wing groups? How much of a coincidence was it that the state and the press in general turned a blind eye?

In the struggle to survive, companies were forced to make tough decisions about which aspect of their operation was most important to them. Was it the show, after all, the product they could sell, which was most important? Was it the class-composition of the audience? Was it the collective principle of organisation? Was getting the 'right line' more important now than ever before? The very wholeness of their operation's opposition to the 'parcel game', the most distinguishing feature of these companies' work, was being fractured. Differences of emphasis became more pronounced.* Instead of drawing closer together, companies became more isolated. Some, where a leadership or management had covertly existed for years, 'came out' in the interests of sound organisation and openly declared themselves as such. Others, whose work had become more and more oriented towards 'good product' effectively took their chance on the open market. Some jettisoned the extra administrative burden of seeking out the more 'difficult' gigs and settled for the relative comfort of the studio-theatre and arts-centre circuit. Others threw content

*Debate was taken up by John McGrath, Gillian Hanna, David Edgar, Michelene Wandor, Bruce Birchall and myself in the pages of *Time Out*, *Theatre Quarterly* (Vol. IX, Nos. 32, 35 & 36, 1980), *Socialist Review* (Issues 1, 2 & 6) and *Platform* (Issues 1, 2 & 4).

out of the window completely and absorbed themselves with finding a 'popular style'. *Everyone did fewer shows.*

As the sense of a 'movement' fragmented, so the inherent contradictions of the groups' situation re-asserted themselves more forcibly. The fact that every company was a small business became more apparent as they were forced to compete with each other for the small pool of subsidy, for the small pool of sufficiently crowd-pulling actors or writers the Fringe had thrown up, for the better London show-cases, for the declining number of gigs offered by the Regional Arts Associations and, most crucially, for the decreasing amount of leisure-money in the population's pockets. Because the 'movement' had never successfully broken out of the ghetto of playing to small audiences in small venues with small subsidy, the 'independence' which had been the by-word of companies in the days of plenty now seemed increasingly fictional. Companies like Red Ladder and the Combination at the Albany, to their credit, attempted to dig further into their local communities – the Albany paying the price by having its national, ACGB grant cut. The Half Moon and Belt and Braces, by taking shows into the West End, attempted to appeal directly to a broader public – Belt and Braces paying the price and getting *its* grant cut. The process of evolving new scripts – either devised by the company or commissioned from writers – had proven a lengthy and labour-consuming task, so people fell back on existing scripts, foreign plays or revivals – anything that took the Terror of the Blank Page from their shoulders.

The innate impatience of the artistic temperament revealed itself. People couldn't wait for the recession, like a rain-storm, to lift. They'd learnt their craft, the emphasis had always been on doing it *now*. Why wait till you're too old and tired? A kind of 'do or die' atmosphere set in. With it, the old antagonism of each theatre skill being pitted against the other returned, and with that, the triumph of the rat, the 'yes-man', the careerist. Throughout the glory days of the Fringe, television and the more established theatres had frequently pillaged it for new ideas and exciting personnel. Writers in particular had moved with considerable fluidity from one to the other, often experiencing the clear-cut production systems of TV and established theatre, for all their lack of intimacy and their control, as a relief from the turmoil of the collectives. For many directors, the relief of a stable production system, good money and some sense of continuity in their work more than compensated for the restraint of being a 'company man' and was certainly an improvement on the lonely and insecure life of the jobbing freelance. For actors, the chance to work on good parts, professionally written, and with fellow actors one could be confident of, learn from and respect, was an important consideration. As the Fringe fragmented, individuals were picked off one by one and often drawn into the Establishment areas of the business, though for some actors the development of a one-person show or cabaret act became a way to keep in work and keep their integrity as well. Because of the huge demands that had been made on them – artistic, personal, political and intellectual – a secure, professional job became a refuge for more than just a few. Artistically, the political Fringe and community theatre, as a *field* of work, had not a lot to offer any more – except perhaps pain. The practitioners had done their bit. The answer now lay in the community itself.

8: SMALL CHANGE, BIG CHANGE

I have attempted to argue in previous chapters that community theatre is not a term descriptive of a particular kind of show or even of work performed at a particular kind of venue; it refers to a model, as yet small-scale, of how the whole of theatre in this country could be brought to relate to the whole of the community and the general social framework within which theatre takes place. To those sceptics who might doubt that the basic 'laws' of showbiz can ever change, I would answer by pointing to the sheer endurance through thick and thin of similar ideals in the past – at the Theatre Royal in Stratford East, the Vic at Stoke, the Liverpool Everyman, and to the tenacity of present companies like the Albany, the Half Moon and Red Ladder in the face of Arts Council cuts, right-wing fire attacks, right-wing reviewers' attacks and recession. Individual artists may find they need to develop faster or in different ways from the theatre companies concerned, but the vision of a more integral relationship between theatre practitioners and their public constantly re-asserts itself.

Enabling the Arts

If further proof were needed of the way in which theatre taste is a developed attribute, of the demand for a certain kind of theatre being created by supply, one need only look at the difference between local authority attitudes towards community theatre fifteen years ago and the present day. In the late sixties and early seventies companies had to struggle to prove their work was not amateur, purely 'propagandistic' or fly-by-night. Now that the 'hidden demand' for this work has been uncovered, some local authorities, even in times of recession, are putting up tens of thousands of pounds to find a suitable company for this area of work. There is also a network of regional and local arts officers anxious to pursue and maintain a sector of cultural activity which has already proved its value to the community. As the Arts Council and the consensus of metropolitan opinion swing backward and away from this area, the rest of the country advances. Above all, there is now a whole generation of audiences for whom their most memorable cultural experience has been the surprise of turning up at a scruffy local hall with no proper seating and no proper stage, and having their preconception of theatre as a bland, sanitised reflection of someone else's world turned completely on its head.

If this demand is to be satisfied and the glimmer of hope which community theatre offers as an alternative to the moribund minority art of the cultural supermarkets realised, the changes of the past fifteen years in the attitude of the community itself to this area of work will have to be scaled up massively. If the boom in the video business and the advent of cable TV are to be prevented from pawning the nation's heartbeat to a handful of marketing experts, substantial levies must be raised from the profits of these businesses – as well as from TV and radio advertising and those areas of broadcasting which prey on the originality and risk-taking of experimental culture. Rather than channel this money through the Arts Council – which has its own priorities and is structured to promote those priorities – the establishment of an Arts Development Fund could ensure that this money reached those regional and experimental initiatives which at present are grossly underfunded. This fund, coupled with the restoration of the Arts Council's Treasury grant to the real level of the mid-seventies, along with measures to ensure the full use of local authorities' 'sixpenny rate' for the arts, could finance a renaissance of arts activity away from the hub of the metropolitan cash-register, which would enable it, potentially, to meet that hidden demand. Even the simple doubling of arts expenditure could effect considerable changes – such is the value for money which the present initiatives of community theatre offer. But in order for that activity to reach and genuinely to reflect the concerns of the mass of the tax-paying population, important structural and administrative changes would also have to occur.

The trap of reproducing simply another minority culture, or remaining 'ghettoised', can only be overcome if the size of performing venues is increased to the point where maximum audience potential can be realised. The trap of a narrow aesthetic vision can only be overcome if companies can afford to employ larger casts and expand production costs. The trap of talent draining towards the metropolitan centre can only be reversed if the quality and excitement of work outside London is maintained and if wage levels are competitive with those in TV and at the national subsidised companies. The trap of good productions disappearing before they maximise their audience, of good scripts not receiving second and third productions in other parts of the country, of a lack of liaison between practitioners and audiences, can only be overcome by doubling the number of those at present engaged in arts administration and by deploying their energies away from the *vetting* of arts initiatives towards the *implementation* of them. At present most administrators within theatre companies and within funding bodies spend at least sixty per cent of their time haggling *with each other* over levels of subsidy. This may be an expression of democracy within the funding process, but it is hardly a democratisation of the arts towards their public. Fixed but guaranteed levels of funding with triennial reviews and annual adjustment might better ensure security and continuity and at the same time enable administrators inside both companies and arts bodies to concentrate on the creative task of getting productions to audiences and vice-versa.

Public and private patrons

The full use of a contribution to the arts from local rates cannot be envisaged without recognising the very hard decisions which many local authorities in under-privileged areas have to face. Housing, hospitals and education all take greater priority in most people's minds. However, the compulsory establishment of arts committees within local authorities would give local activists a lobby through which to press their claims, while the establishment of a national arts development purse which they could appeal to would give such committees an incentive and the chance to demonstrate the actual benefits of an arts policy; and as this money would not be 'local' money it would not seem like 'robbing Peter to pay Paul'.

Once the arts are on a sound financial and administrative footing nationally, the relation of cultural institutions to industry can be tackled on a dignified basis. At present the level of recognition by industry of its social responsibility towards the arts is pitifully low. Whether cultural enterprises approach business or trade unions, they are placed in the position of poor relation with a begging bowl. This encourages industry to respond to these approaches with the attitude 'What's in it for us?' and subsequently to answer their own question in the crudest, materialist terms. Culture becomes yet again a sales point for banks, tobacco companies, electronics firms or – rarely – the labour movement. Only from a position of strength can a theatre company receive financial help from business and still maintain a balance within society of its material and cultural emphases. Only the National Theatre and the Royal Shakespeare Company can at present seriously look an industrial sponsor in the eye and make the sponsor feel as lucky to be sponsoring them as the theatre is to receive the sponsorship. Only when businesses are desperate to climb on the bandwagon of a burgeoning, national, cultural renaissance, will the same relationship obtain for smaller companies. But no form of institutional sponsorship should ever contribute to the *continuing* operation of cultural enterprises. The responsibility for revenue subsidy must remain with the state. Sponsorship is a splendid way for industry to demonstrate its social responsibility towards culture on a once-off or capital endowment basis, but the moment it plays a part in the *running* of the arts, the arts will be compromised. (A wonderful example of this danger was a company in the South-West who, short of money, sought sponsorship from a local tobacco firm. To their surprise they were offered a revenue grant of £15,000 – at that time enough to run the company for a year. The only condition was that the company change its name to that of a famous brand of cigarette!)

A similar awareness of the dangers of patronage should be brought to the composition of boards and committees governing arts funding and the management of theatre companies. The fact that knowledge, experience and expertise in the *traditional* arts rests mainly with the upper-middle class is largely irrelevant to an arts policy which takes seriously the problem of generating a culture crossing all class barriers. A working-class Tory housewife might be more representative of audience demand on a local arts committee, a theatre board or its list of 'patrons' than a middle-class socialist with a lifetime of experience in semi-subsidised theatre. The defensiveness with which arts administration approaches what it perceives as 'philistinism' is a recipe for an atrophied and inward-looking culture becoming increasingly distant from the public it is supposed to serve. Only the creative artists and staff working in theatres can make a new culture *happen*, and they should always have a controlling interest in the management of their company's operation. Only when they have that freedom and 'space' to operate can they relax to take on board the demands that the community places on them. The way those demands are channelled should be as fully representative as possible of the community they come from. Consumer and trade union representation are the most desperately under-encouraged aspect of community involvement in our present arts establishment. Since the state is the ultimate manager of arts funds, it is there that the responsible 'control' of public funds should lie, not in the day-to-day running of the company. And that state control should also be as representative as possible.

A new commitment

However important the imagination is to the internal world of the theatre, it counts as yet for very little in the community at large. And in the *English* community at large, being an almost uniquely pragmatic, materialist, insular and philistine people, the arts count for even less. For community theatre practitioners, therefore, it is one thing to *imagine* a theatre company functioning as a valuable and integral part of a local community, it is quite another thing for that to be put into practice. However strong the *will* amongst artists committed to this field of work to 'relate' to the community, they remain first and foremost artists. Their principal desire is to act in, direct or write plays, and they will remain linked into the demands of their profession unless extraordinarily propitious circumstances determine otherwise. The acting profession is, after all, essentially peripatetic. The commonest pattern of life for an actor is to live in London (where it's easier to audition for TV, the two big national companies, the West End and even many regional companies); to work away from home only for short periods, and to be constantly moving from job to job. In the terms of local authority job definitions, this is 'casual labour'. It's a far cry from growing up and going to school in a particular area, taking up an apprenticeship there and eventually getting a secure job with the same firm for thirty years with a pension at the end, which is the norm aspired to (though in fact rarely achieved) in many working-class communities.

The point here is that it is rare for theatre workers, and actors in particular, to be in a position to commit their *whole* lives to a community in the way that people stuck there (willingly or not) have to. However great a company's commitment to the *job*, it will always seem to the community that actors are fly-by-night people, here today and gone tomorrow, leading glamorous and affluent (!) lives, with no real concern for the struggles of people 'on the ground'. However great the commitment of theatre practitioners to the *principle* of their work, there is always a grain of truth in this view of them. Many people do, after all, go into theatre and its concomitant risks to escape the humdrum, nine-to-five world, to enjoy variety and grasp opportunities which others might envy but would not dare give up their security for; but it contributes less to the cementing of relations between the theatre world and the community at large to insist piously that acting is a job of work like any other, with its own trade union and labour problems, than to spend time in a community, put down roots and participate shoulder-to-shoulder in the struggles of that community. Just as a business sponsor will want to know what's in it for him, a community requires palpable proof *in its own terms* that these fly-by-night people are committed to them before they commit their own hearts, minds and energies to supporting their artists.

And it's not just the *name* of the theatre company, or its administrator or director, that need to maintain a high profile within the community. However much more customary it is for directors and administrators to 'represent' their company within the community, the actors are what the public sees. They are the visible and palpable part of the operation, the end of it through which the public identifies with the play and the work of the company as a whole. It's the actors who arouse admiration and generate mystery. If a company wishes to become a 'familiar' part of the community, the actors' role in this is all-important, just as seeing the same actors in different roles from week to week was part of the charm of fortnightly rep.

This audience identification with actors does not recommend the widespread current practice amongst regional repertory theatres of actors working on short-term contracts, being hired and fired by an invisible, hierarchical management. On the other hand the maintenance of a permanent company also has its problems. The chances of finding the right sort of plays with casts which exactly fit the company are very slim. Even with a company of reasonable size and a good balance in terms of age and sex, the tendency would be to fall back on the known and well-worn classics. A healthy programme of commissioning new plays is one way around this problem, but asking writers to create a play in order to fix a logistical problem of scheduling or personnel is the wrong way to go about it.

Where the principal intent, then, is to respond through the *content* of a company's programme of work to the needs of its immediate community, to demonstrate a commitment to it, maintain a dialogue and a familiar presence, the actor becomes increasingly important, as does the playwright. And, as the link between script and performer, the director's function assumes a new importance – as does design (the other principal element which is visible and palpable to the audience). Instead of the prima donna director, agent of the managerial hierarchy and instigator of a production 'concept', and instead of a design with a will of its own, the collaborative cohesion of all the company's varied skills is required in order that its work achieve a clear identity within the community. Each and every theatre skill has to redefine its function in relation to the demands of a new audience.

Given a situation where employment for theatre workers is no longer principally a matter of catching the 'right person's' eye on the road to grander and more exciting parts – preferably with national subsidised companies in London – the importance of the 'here and now' increases. No longer prey to the 'Next Job Syndrome', no longer a victim of someone else's interpretation of what the audience wants, engaging with that audience directly both on stage and through the company's policy, theatre workers also take on an increased responsibility. It is no longer enough for an actor to think simply and exclusively about the part he's playing; the relation of that part to the production as a whole, and of the production to the repertoire and its audience become crucial questions. Similarly for writers and directors, it is no longer enough to think exclusively about the production in hand; consideration of both the acting company and the company's whole operation in the community become vital. Instead of one's environment being an irrelevance and the future being an unknown quantity which the present show is propelling you towards, environment and future are brought to bear on the present job in hand.

But whereas the jobs of writers, directors and designers necessarily carry with them a certain responsibility for the whole production while granting to other artists a measure of independence in their work, an actor's primary point of engagement is with his or her own part while being subject to everyone else's input. Writers and directors who also act frequently comment on the relief they feel when their only responsibility is for their own performance. Actors who direct or write comment on their enjoyment of the additional control over their work which this brings. But the generally accepted 'rights and responsibilities' of these various functions can lead to a number of subjective fallacies. Because they're responsible for the *overall* production, it's possible for writers and directors to assume they're being 'objective' when in fact they are simply exercising their own individual skill. For actors, the objective recognition that they're at the 'sharp end' of performance yet remain the passive vehicle of others' vision can lead to the desire to substitute performance for creativity – whether by believing that a good play is one that has equally satisfying parts for the whole company, or that the only good play is one that gives you the chance to show off the full range of your acting skills. It's vital therefore that people in collective companies learn not to confuse the subjective interests of their function inside the production system with the ultimate and long-term purpose of the company's relation to the community. Increased participation in the content of shows, in the company's repertoire and its operation in the community is the most important way in which the interests of particular skills can become collectively focussed rather than compounding the already existing sense of actors as a passive and exploitable race apart. |

Democracy cuts both ways

The dilemma this poses for theatre workers in practical terms is considerable. How 'democratic' in fact is a so-called 'collective' theatre company? For trade unionists in a mixed economy the use of public money in a nationalised industry does not necessarily 'socialise' it. The extent to which both consumers and workers actually reap the benefit of collective or state intervention is perhaps the extent to which 'participation' or workers' control within management may be embraced. Similarly, the extent to which actors and other theatre workers can be required to subordinate their subjective interests to the 'collective' good depends entirely on the degree to which the company's work is genuinely 'socialised'. It's quite possible, for example, for certain members of a group to be more articulate and persuasive than others and to dominate the group as effectively as an actual 'boss'. It's also possible for a company to work in a broadly co-operative way but for certain decisions to be the preserve of a small group. It's even possible for a company to operate within itself in a totally democratic way with no division of labour and yet in fact to be employed (as sometimes happens with theatre-in-education companies and young people's theatres) by the 'main house' management of a repertory theatre, which in turn is of course controlled by a conventional board, which in turn is subject to the scrutiny of the Arts Council. However 'collectively' theatre workers behave in this situation, however much responsibility they take on their own shoulders for the company's whole operation, their work is ultimately liable to be used by that management and, indeed, the Arts Council. The actors, after all, can be sacked, but the board and the Arts Council can point to the good work that sacked company has done in the community. The fact that 'main houses' often use such companies as an alibi for the lack of social connectedness in their own operation makes this danger more than just a matter of nit-picking definition. It can lead to disillusionment and cynicism amongst theatre workers about *all* efforts towards democratisation.

Given the difficulties described in previous chapters of immediate and wholesale attempts at 'collectivisation', it would be foolish to prescribe that all theatre companies should be run in a purely collective way. Many people feel more comfortable and function better within recognised structures. Where such structures are frankly acknowledged and willingly accepted, they can even work in the better interest of all concerned. Sometimes in rehearsal, for example, a company can get stuck in a rut. This benefits no one. A director standing 'outside' this process can perceive the problem and either play a trick on a company or set up an improvisation where a company *discovers for itself* the way out of the rut. This works to everyone's advantage, but it would be difficult indeed for a company to play a trick on itself or spontaneously discover the way out of a rut if it had just consciously voted to do so! Given this difficulty in 'seeing oneself' from outside, the value of community and audience representation on boards and in the figure of the director can be seen in practical terms as well as those of democratic principle.

Many companies attempt in any case to increase the degree of democratic involvement of both company and community within conventional structures. In this instance the value lies in a clear chain of authority which can actually free people to get on with the job in hand while ways are found – say through company and public meetings – to re-examine the efficacy of the given method of organisation. Provided this is accompanied by a commitment to increased democracy for both practitioners and public, it can serve to re-educate all parties towards a better understanding of how they inter-relate. Whether collectively or hierarchically organised, every link in the chain of control and communication – from the public and its purse through the responsibilities of internal management to the mounting of productions and their dialogue back to the public – needs to be adequate to both the tougher, material realities of a company's situation and to the release of creative potential within it.

If, for example, the Arts Council were to be democratised, it would first have to be recognised that it receives its money from the population as a whole but disburses it on behalf of the *state*, which is something entirely different. Under pluralistic political control, any state management of the arts has to recognise the interests of both producers and consumers. It also has a responsibility both to satisfy immediate demands and to look to the future. It has both to rediscover and continue the best traditions of the past and to encourage new developments. The fact that producers at present constantly clamour at its doors for money, to which its response (apart from acknowledging its chronic shortage of the stuff) is only to point to an *interpretation* of what the consumer wants, is a sad indication of its present social imbalance and passivity. A clear and firm brief, representative of a wider spectrum of social interests and vigorously pursued, could turn a defensive and stagnant 'guardian of the public purse' into a wise and productive public investor.

Similarly with theatre management: for a more *engaged* public response to theatre, a more *engaging* management policy needs to be pursued. Television may be soporific, but it gives value for money. The special strengths of theatre, its directness, immediacy and flesh-and-blood openness, need to be played to. Where local public money is added to state money, those strengths should be placed at the service of a management policy which can be seen and felt by local audiences to be of direct and immediate interest. While only the artists and theatre staff themselves can implement such a policy, and should therefore control it, the involvement and engagement of the local community should be actively sought and responded to. Contact between theatre practitioners and their public, from performance through public meeting to boardroom discussion, should be the dominant factor in shaping policy. Whether the work is then produced under a conventional artistic director or some form of collective artistic leadership, the principal criterion is that it should respond to this perceived audience demand.

9: VOICING THE CONNECTIONS

Once audiences are brought into active consideration in the kinds of ways suggested in the preceding chapter, many of the either/or debates which have raged within recent years concerning a more democratic arts policy then become resolvable. Should one 'bring art to the people' or support the art that people make for themselves? Should an artistic policy have one, distinctive 'voice' or reflect a variety of interests and approaches? Should theatre acknowledge its artifice, lay its cards on the table and be honestly anti-illusionistic, or adhere to a realism to which actor and audience can more easily relate? Questions of internal organisation are also more easily answered when the context within which they're asked is known. Is it better to have a permanent company where practitioners can become more familiar with each other's work processes and fit the practitioners to the plays? Does a policy which guarantees security of employment offer greater chances of a satisfactory artistic product for an audience than one which provides for artists to come and go according to that all-important ingredient, enthusiasm? Does a policy of positive discrimination in employing company members who are working-class, women or from ethnic minorities necessary guarantee that the product will serve the long-term interests of such under-represented sections of the community? Where amateurs and professionals work alongside each other, do the advantages of their respective qualities (freshness and immediacy in amateurs, polish and skill in professionals) emerge more forcibly than the disadvantages (amateurs apeing the worst foibles of 'the business', professionals 'flattening' their own delivery)?

The only practical way through this maze of contradictory considerations is for companies to have clearly stated executive policies in response to their audiences' perceived demand. 'Clearly stated' because that audience demand will change. Live performance and a public which is actively represented in a company's policy-making will mean that a constant two-way process of learning is going on, a process that doesn't begin and end with the rise and fall of what used to be a curtain. 'Perceived' demand because, as argued in an earlier chapter, however an audience's demands are voiced, the way in which they're understood and translated into a product depends on a multitude of subjective factors.

Neither community nor theatre will achieve a dialogue based on mutual interest simply by wishing it. The experience or hopes of a community cannot be transformed overnight into a satisfactory aesthetic event simply by being voiced. The translation of that 'voice' into a product or a policy depends in the first instance on who is seen to represent it *vis-à-vis* the theatre company. Who are the people from the community who have most frequent contact with the theatre, how representative are they of either the community at large or the company's actual or intended audience? Given that such community representatives do broadly reflect its 'voice', in what matter should they frame the demands they make on their theatre company? It is as unsatisfactory for community 'representatives' to give a theatre a shopping-list of demands as it is for the theatre company simply to do the shows it feels like doing anyway and expect the community to respond gratefully. Every statement or action by the one side will almost certainly be picked up and interpreted slightly differently by the other. Sometimes, tragically, it will even be interpreted in quite the opposite sense. Both sides therefore have to learn to listen to each other and understand some of the background and the processes from which each other's contribution to the dialogue arises. The concerns of a trades council, for example, will need to be understood as much in terms of the past and present struggles of the labour movement as the concerns of a theatre company need to be understood in terms of subsidy, staffing levels and creative resources. From the original idea for a show through to the product an audience sees, there are a hundred and one connections to be made – between the community and its representation to the company, between the company and its relation to a writer, between writer and director, between director and actors, between performers and audience, and finally between actual audience and 'public reception' as defined by reviews, conversation or gossip about the show, letters to newspapers, response of funding bodies, etc. If this process is to be productive, each of these connections requires a certain sensitivity from each party towards the other as well as an alert and consistent, critical rigour. Clarity and firmness of resolve need to be coupled with sensitivity and flexibility in practice.

Leaders and led

'Firmness of resolve' can of course very quickly lead to autocracy. How can the former be guaranteed without the latter becoming a danger? How can the state, a theatre company's policy-making body or a director on the rehearsal floor with actors, actively bring to expression the full richness and variety, the full creative potential held within our society? Whether that resolve is individual or collective, it has to be acknowledged that in any walk of life, any human activity, there is a line of authority – sometimes thin, sometimes invisible – between leaders and led, those who assume social responsibility for an activity and those whose principal responsibility is only to themselves. Whether it's a youth worker with a bunch of kids, a director on the rehearsal floor or someone in a personal relationship who, say, has an idea for decorating the home, the spur to action comes from one quarter, its implementation from another. However narrow the dividing line, instigation is one thing, response is another. Even if they alternate, you cannot do both at once. Any teacher who has tried to 'democratise' the teaching process will know that, ultimately, that line of authority does not have a point of balance. Ask a class-room what it would like to do today and either no clear idea emerges or a leader does. Sit in a roomful of people where potential leaders with positive, creative ideas are 'holding back', and the result is stagnation. However great the sympathy, understanding and generosity between the two sides, you have to be on one or the other. Creative initiative is a fence which can't be sat on.

Once you cross the line, your attitudes change. The more you lead and others follow, the more you develop the wisdom and prejudices of leaders. The more you follow, the greater your knowledge and prejudice about being led. For this to happen, however, both sides need the other. Willingness to 'give and take' in these situations is conditioned by how satisfying the respective positions of leader and led are to both parties. Leadership only lasts as long as it works and is credible. In business and political life leadership frequently changes hands according to people's perception of their common situation. But it only changes hands satisfactorily if a credible alternative presents itself. So-called 'power-struggles' are, in this sense, nothing more than the working through of social necessity. It's important therefore and part of their responsibility that leaders are not blind to the predicament of the led. They need to realise that their actions have provoked and will provoke reactions. The led, in turn, should be conscious of the responsibilities borne by the leaders. Only in this way can the two complementary roles function harmoniously. A social awareness of leadership therefore implies necessarily not only that the actions of leaders be beneficial to the led, but that they also enable alternative leaders to emerge in the same collective interest. The initiative in personal relationships can often change from partner to partner, and the knowledge each has of the other can lend this process a smooth transition. In the pursuit of an arts policy at national or local level, and indeed for individual theatre companies within the community, this kind of social awareness is vital. Recognition that no policy can be democratic unless it is stated has to be coupled with the genuinely representative structure that will regenerate it. Recognition that artists and practitioners necessarily 'lead the way' in the actual provision of culture has to be coupled with structures that ensure a productive dialogue with consumers. And within theatre companies themselves the flexibility for individual imaginative initiatives to emerge and be followed should not be shut off.

The fullest possible consultation of all parties involved, the broadest possible statement of common aims, provided this is linked and leads to the action expressive of these processes, are crucial to closing the gap in our divided culture.

Who inspires who?

This implies a completely new dynamic behind the funding and administration of the arts. At present we have a competitive system where 'making it', 'upstaging' and the star system are by-words because wealth is the carrot dangled *ahead* of people. Consequently the less obvious, more delicate, more complicated forms of art get trampled in the rush. Often the product of the greatest contradictions and tensions in our society, the value of these forms is frequently recognised too late. To live those tensions, to feel them deeply and understand them fully is to be socially disarmed. The truer the artist in this sense, the less power she has. Once the expression of those tensions and contradictions lodges in people's minds, they are no longer a private matter. Having sprung from a social source, they return to a social stream. Artists of this kind are mere mediators whose work can be chewed up and spat out by society at any time. A genuinely social arts policy would therefore recognise the social value of this kind of art by putting its wealth *behind* its artists. It would *release* art to fulfil its social function by providing finance to overcome the logistic problems of bringing product and consumer together. The incentives of being understood and recognised – still the most meaningful to serious artists – would remain, but recognition would be by a different public and by means of criteria no longer based on the twin insults of market and cultural elite. The task of state, local community, management and even the director in rehearsal would be to *clear the way* for the true dialogue between practitioners and public.

An illustration of the complex and uneasy relation between the social and administrative context of art and the personal and aesthetic concerns of artists is given in Andrzej Wajda's film *The Conductor*. In it, John Gielgud plays a world famous conductor who, having left his native Poland as a young man, returns in old age to give a concert in a provincial town. The daughter of a woman he had an affair with in those days now plays in the orchestra and the daughter provides the substantial interest of the film. Whereas the young conductor ambitiously and urgently – even desperately – works and works his orchestra to get them up to international scratch, Gielgud swans in and, seemingly without effort – through his sheer love of and absorption in the music – raises the orchestra's performance, their own level of enjoyment, and makes friends of them all. Though he's known to be temperamental and we see that in private he is neurotic about the state of both his mind and body, none of this is shown to the orchestra. The crunch comes when the Party organisers of the concert begin to interfere. Because the concert is to be recorded and may therefore become prestigious internationally, the young conductor is prevailed upon to introduce top-notch Warsaw musicians into the orchestra to 'raise' its performance. Gielgud is happy to play to workers in a factory hall, but as he raises the baton to conduct a pre-performance rehearsal, he realises he has different musicians and walks out.

The sense of 'return' is crucial to this story. The famous man returns to his roots. In doing so he is both reviewing his own life and striving for a sense of personal completeness. But at the same time he is 'giving back' a part of himself to the community which bore him. This gesture is not lost on the orchestra, who quickly learn to share his self-absorption in the music, or on his audience who at the end of the film form a massive queue covering the street-kerbs for hundreds of metres. 'Instruction by example' is another important theme. The conductor doesn't lead by singling out individuals or criticising particular sections but by inviting them to share his pleasure in those sections which go well. There is an almost oriental emphasis here on the way in which a subjective state of mind can influence objective performance. Rather than objectify the faults of particular musicians and watch them disable themselves with obsessive anxiety about specific problems, he overcomes difficulties by, as it were, ignoring them, by demonstrating personally the emotional 'key' which unlocks the problem. He *enables* his orchestra to perform better by offering a positive example rather than disabling them with negative criticism.

This enablement is achieved through pleasure and enthusiasm, qualities which can't be taught – and therefore corrupted – by a hierarchical separation of those who 'get it right' from those who don't. Sharing and experiencing are paramount. The pursuit of such consummate public pleasure however leaves the famous man inadequate in his own personal life and destroys the young couple's relationship. Having deserted the mother to pursue his ideal, he returns to awaken the ideal in the daughter but similarly fails to relate to the upset he causes in her personal life. In the end he does not give the concert but dies sitting in the queue of fans. Questions about these 'real-life' relationships are, one suspects, as important to Wajda's themes as the interference of the authorities.

Return to sender

The sense of 'return', then, is central to the idea behind community theatre. Not only for a generation of theatre workers from working-class origins, anxious to enjoy that sense of completeness in the exercise of their art within their own inherited culture which is generally enjoyed in the West only by the sons and daughters of the cultureaucracy, but also in the strict, economic sense of a return on that portion of working-class people's taxes which at present subsidises middle-class bums on the seats of our insulated and precious arts establishments. Simply to erect the buildings (as in the sixties) or 'allow' small groups to experiment in this field is not enough.

Every aspect of the circuitous and hazardous route by which a people generates and receives its culture needs to be directed energetically towards the end of returning its own culture to the people. Those who sit aloof in the air-conditioned, centrally-heated offices of our universities, publishing houses and arts-funding bodies may wonder what, if any, culture exists 'down there' to be returned. But theatre practitioners who have frozen and choked in the sooty air of the cultural slums know first-hand that where the human spirit is still able to rise above the sheer physical exhaustion of the mines or the building sites, the mind-numbing onslaught of the production line, the drudgery of routine or the humiliation of the bottom rung in the pecking order, the richness of experience and degree of perception it can possess about human character and personality, the robust sense of style and dignity it can demonstrate, and the sheer originality of its self-expression, all exceed by far the stale, narrow, bland and derivative world of our received culture. It is not lack of technique or expertise which primarily prevents the satisfactory expression of that culture within our society, but the very channels of expression themselves which exist there at present. You have only to look at the number of artists in British theatre today who started their professional careers with Unity Theatre, Joan Littlewood, Stoke – or now, increasingly, the touring companies and venues of the political and fringe theatre – to appreciate the energy and vivacity which lies just beneath the surface of our cultural life and can be released by an initiative that genuinely cares.

You have also only to look at what happens to kids in drama workshops at community centres to see the deleterious effect of our cultural channels on the 'natural' talents and abilities generated within working-class culture. As soon as the prospect of 'escape' from an immediate, dulling environment is held forth, the temptation to conform to the values of the dominant culture is irresistible. Even if it goes against the grain (as it does for many), the prospect of economic 'betterment' in the brassier sections of showbiz or of artistic 'improvement' in the rarefied atmosphere of the minority culture is not merely a temptation but a condition of survival. If you want to stay out of the cold and grime, you either embrace those values, or else you disappear from sight. ⫽

It isn't then just new buildings or a new product – new shows – which are required, it is a new market-place; or rather not a market-place at all but the abolition of the market-place and the instant return of its culture to the population as a whole. Why should working-class people pay to see performers who've been abducted from their own culture revitalising bourgeois culture? Only when ordinary people have completely free access to the places of performance as both producers and consumers, when the divide of the box-office is totally irrelevant, will the possibility of a genuinely popular culture exist.

The likelihood, however, of a totally free culture in the near future is hardly great. Nor would it necessarily be valued in a society where the worth of a commodity or an experience is pre-judged by its price. Audiences might well believe that the cheaper or freer a performance is, the less worthwhile it is. Community companies who have pitched their prices low in order not to discriminate against the poor have encountered this difficulty. The alternative – of concessions for the unemployed, students, pensioners and unionised members of the theatrical profession – begins to smack of a two-tier culture. The very fact that a cultural event is judged in advance by its ticket-price tells us a great deal about how our society relates to its culture. Obviously these are values which cannot be changed by culture alone – although the establishment of a few large, bustling, smart but not overpowering community and arts centres by some Regional Arts Associations offers as great a physical example of this prospect as any cultural initiative can presently achieve. Values generally would have to change, however, before purely cultural initiatives could go substantially further in this direction. But the impotence of culture on its own in this regard should not mean that our thinking about it is led and dominated by market values. At present our Arts Council and other funding bodies *insist* that a certain proportion of companies' revenue comes from their box-office receipts. The value of many companies' work is judged on this basis, thus discriminating against companies who play to the poor or put effort into playing to the 'hidden demand' audiences which are difficult to find. How many *artistic* decisions are consequently taken by theatre managements on the grounds of likely *box-office* takings? This slavish adherence to the laws of the market-place has never and will never generate a vital national culture. It will do no more than reproduce the values which already exist. All shows will tend towards the values of *No sex please we're British, Star Wars, Emmanuelle, Crossroads* or even, it has to be said, *Nicholas Nickleby*: the vacuous, the violent, the salacious, the banal or the re-hash.

Subsidy is therefore not just a piecemeal necessity but an across-the-board prerequisite of any genuine culture. Realistically – until people the world over find a value-system independent of money – there has to be a balance between patronage and box-office takings. But that balance is not something that can be imposed in percentage terms across the board. The purpose of subsidy, besides enabling good production standards, should be directed towards the huge social and administrative effort needed to redress the cultural imbalance in our society. The danger exists of course for both community companies and conventional subsidised companies of enjoying the extra time which subsidy buys and forgetting about the audience completely. A social arts policy, funded by public money, can only justify this kind of artistic licence if the pleasure it gives artists is eventually shared by their public. The trap of identifying box-office takings as a measure of public enjoyment and therefore as a means of 'policing' arts funding is nonetheless wholly inappropriate. Only when the mass of the population are in a position sensibly to judge whether the culture they are paying for is their own will proper criteria exist.

It would take an arts policy which itself 'led by example' to put this situation right. If Wajda's conductor achieves more by generously tolerating the weaker members of his orchestra in favour of his own and everyone's increased pleasure at their concerted effort, the faults of a subsidy system where administrators on both sides of its wall spend 60 per cent of their time in nit-picking haggling are self-evident. The aim must be to *release* the nation's artistic resources.

10: ALTOGETHER NOW

Provided adequate economic and administrative support exists, and that its exercise is qualitatively informed by considerations peculiar to the production of culture of the kind outlined in the previous chapter, the possibility of theatre genuinely becoming a vital part of its community comes a little closer. 'Scaling-up' in terms of seating capacity is important not only in order for companies drawing full houses to take advantage of their success and have a real measure of economic independence, but also to make their presence in the community more strongly felt. In this latter respect the use of the auditorium not only by the acting company but also by amateur companies, by locally and nationally known musicians and as a meeting-place for tenants, trade union groups and other community organisations is important. Large enough to be prominent in the community, but not so large as to be impersonal, its use for other purposes will inevitably colour the way in which its audience receives the product presented in it.

This familiarity needs to be accompanied by technical flexibility. A restrictive proscenium-arch auditorium would not only limit the kind of theatre produced within it, it would also impose a certain style on the other cultural activities it housed. The same goes for the general context within which the auditorium is situated. The more this resembles a veritable rabbit warren of cultural activity, with workshops, rehearsal spaces, formal meeting-places and informal ones like cafés, bars, bookstalls, printing-shops, nurseries and so on, the greater the feeling there will be around the building of a general cultural meeting-place, familiar and accessible to the wider community.

Oval House in Kennington, London, has followed this approach for many years, and the recently opened Tom Allen Centre in Stratford, London, also has something of this quality. Other arts and community centres up and down the country – the Borough Hall at Stafford is a memorable example – have demonstrated in recent years the value of this multi-activity approach. Flexible staging and a wide variety of activities, however, pose problems of programming and logistics. For the activities to run to full advantage, adequate technical and administrative staff are essential not only to ensure the smooth running and integration of activities but also a genuine sense of their availability. It's no good spending huge amounts of money on expensive and sophisticated hardware if it can never be used, nor in creating a 'rabbit warren' if half its corridors are closed. The employment of local people with a genuine desire to see facilities *used* and an openness which will encourage the shy and hesitant can only enhance this accessibility.

It isn't only in the technical and administrative side that the active participation of local people should be sought. The exaggeration and aggravation of any existing gap between 'professionals' and 'amateurs', between the local and metropolitan, between 'main house' (a terrible term) and studio or touring activities will only serve to reinforce existing cultural prejudices and perpetuate the division betweeen 'high' culture (with all its questionable 'standards') and the rest. We've already seen a drift towards a similar division in the relation between 'main houses' in regional repertory theatres and studio theatres to which new, experimental and children's work is frequently relegated. The whole acting company should be free to move from one area of work to the other, and the traditional six days per week of performance should be similarly broken up to open the auditorium for talks, meetings and concerts, particularly in the early part of the week, thus freeing the company to go *out* into the community or to use their skills as educators in workshops and talks, further breaking up the sense of monolithic distance between the company's repertoire and its public. In this relationship it's also important that full-time employed artists are not seen always and inevitably to be enjoying exclusively the best opportunities and facilities available. If the creative stimulus their work offers is to be backed up by genuine and productive encouragement, it's important that young people, amateurs and indeed visiting artists also get a crack of the whip.

Opening out

With such an abundance and diversity of activity, the intimacy of a closely-knit collaborative group will inevitably suffer – though it is possible for this to continue *within* the overall framework. Where that intimacy produces only inward-looking, 'hothouse' reflexes, however, this is perhaps no bad thing. The exposure of a company's working life to a degree of 'outside' contact – even to the extent of public rehearsal – can be useful provided it is approached for the refreshing new insights it can offer rather than feared as an inhibiting inconvenience. It will, after all, be essential in such 'public' circumstances that individual artists can enjoy those conditions of private contemplation and exercise which are the incubators of their imaginative and technical skills.

The relation between individuals' creative needs and full public participation in the life of the company can finally be achieved only by the delegation of certain responsibilities to mandated representatives, with possibly a system of rotating representation to ensure that everyone's voice is not only represented but heard actually and in person from time to time. It is not enough for only the customary custodians of public interest – the general managers, artistic directors, local councillors, trade union officers, local arts officers and representatives of tenants', women's, educational and ethnic minority organisations (all well-versed in traditional 'meeting-ese') to deliberate on the running of the whole operation. Typists, actors, technicians, local authority workers, teachers, shop stewards, school pupils and the public themselves should also be heard in person if the executive body of the company is not to become simply an abstract forum for in-fighting amongst conflicting interest-groups. Without the direct input of those whose work is affected daily by the executive's decisions it will stultify into a pale reflection of our present-day theatre boards, where those who sit on them know little about day-to-day practice and those who don't know little about their board.

There will inevitably be conflict – between the company and the community, between the administration and the artists, between finance and everyone else, between 'insiders' and 'outsiders' of every kind. The importance of explicitness and of the ability to listen in these situations will become more important than ever. If the value of live theatre over and against other media lies in all its participants having at least the opportunity to look each other in the eye at every stage of its development, that value must surely have a place in its administration as well.

Leading from behind

The aim of artists working within such a radically restructured theatre world and concerned to reflect a genuinely popular culture, would have to be correspondingly generous. There is a sense in which a 'lead' is as much expected from artists as from the authorities. Not necessarily a lead in the avant-garde sense, rather that if everyone has a germ of aesthetic appreciation in them but only a few are able to pursue it professionally, then those who are unable would rather see something 'special' emanate from artists than a merely banal reflection of the parameters of their own existence. Wajda's conductor is, after all, expected to 'raise' the level of his orchestra. This is an integral function of art but one of which, because it is grossly misapplied in our society, many community theatre workers are suspicious. Usually it is seen in class terms: we talk of 'high' art, 'standards of excellence', moving 'up' the scale of grant awards, 'raised consciousness', 'heightened awareness', and so on. By contrast, much radical thinking about the arts emphasises the 'grass roots' and how it feels 'on the ground' – in some ways merely reinforcing the renowned British 'upstairs, downstairs' mentality. But it is not only in Britain that such attitudes prevail, and while art is certainly somewhat more ethereal than a nine-to-five existence, its source is inside people rather than halfway to heaven. Our language is hopelessly inadequate to describe the processes involved – one reason why so much confusion and controversy surrounds its manufacture – but the purpose of a genuinely popular art must surely be to draw out those qualities which exist in everyone, to 'educate' in the sense of the original Latin *educare*,* while remembering that the most successful learning is usually that which is *enjoyed*.

Some community companies in the seventies suffered however from directors or leading figures who seemed to assume their function was to lead not by example but by a sense of moral superiority. Some socialist companies even assumed this sense towards their audience. There is no fundamental difference in this attitude from that which decided the nascent Arts Council should take Greek tragedy to 'the workers'. Most people reckon they know about *something* better than others – and good for them! – but the unforgivable sin is to *assume* that you do. One of the great and (I suspect wilfully) perpetual misconceptions about Brecht is that the pedagogic element in his work is equated with this kind of patronising arrogance. In fact Brecht's *Lehrstücke* emanated from a desire to share his own enthusiastic discovery of the methods of Marxism, and there was always the sense in his work – more fully realised in the later plays – of measuring the lessons of experience against the yardstick of conscious analysis. His method strived to reflect that of the scientific hypothesis tested against the proofs of the physical world. In that sense it was profoundly modest. And since his hypothesis was stated from the beginning, leaving the audience to make up its own mind, his method was also more honest than that of many of our contemporary media-manipulators who profess to deal in 'realism' or to 'simply show the facts and ask questions only', but in fact cook the argument from beginning to end.

There is nothing inherently misguided, then, about forms of theatre which are explicit, state their ground-rules or proceed from a declared position. Far greater is the totalitarianism of a 'realistic' approach which takes a slice of life, pins it down and implies 'That's the way things are.' If the aim is to offer material which will take root, grow and expand in people's memories and imaginations, that material has to possess the volatility which the characters and situations in Brecht's work had even at their

*To lead out.

most explicit. They should be able to go in several directions. It's worth noting that the situations in even the most 'didactic' of the *Lehrstücke* like *The Exception and the Rule* or *The Measures Taken* were perhaps more volatile than those anywhere else in his work. The leadership of art which makes its thinking available and leaves its audience's options open is infinitely more democratic than one which hugs its cards to its chest in order to wrap the game up.

By similar means community theatre possesses the potential to lift the lid off a number of volatile issues which the established theatre, locked into its box-office system, its hierarchical management and its 'realism', cannot hope to deal with. To present those issues as if we knew the answer from beginning to end is to kill that potential stone dead. Wajda's conductor succeeded precisely by *not* haranguing his orchestra but by plunging immediately into what gave him 'lift-off' and hoping they'd follow. If the source of our sense of 'other world' is within all of us, we need to 'get into' it – concentration, enthusiasm, risk, experiment, research – before we can 'get off' on it.

Community theatre gives a lead in this direction in that the first question it asks itself is 'How do we "get into" the lives of the people in our area?' The question is dangerous but less impersonal than the conventional 'What do they want?' The difference lies in the attempt to get beyond the static estimation of a show's ability to 'pull' an audience next week, and towards a dynamic understanding of the relationship between producers and audience in the long term. Since many of the audience needs addressed by community theatre are hidden, the response, when it comes, is to a rare experience. Comments like 'I didn't think theatre was like this, there's so much in it, I want to see it again' or 'I never thought politics was any of my business, but I see now that if you don't busy yourself with it, it'll busy itself with you' or 'I never thought I'd see my own life, the things I care and worry about every day, up on stage, acted out' are typical within my own experience and that of colleagues in the same field. The degree of confirmation, of 'lift' and sheer self-respect that audiences can gain from a theatre which concerns itself with the stuff of their own lives cannot be achieved through other media, or through a theatre viewed as distant and separate. ('A focken insult' as one Glaswegian shop-steward described an expensive trip 'up west' to see a long-running comedy, or 'nothing to do with what the play was about' as one teacher described a production of Brecht at one of our national subsidised houses.)

11: ART ALWAYS COMES LAST

The fact that theatre is produced under conditions where those involved are in each other's immediate presence gives a clue not only to its democratic potential as a form of communication – the realisation of the imagination's 'free zone' in actuality – but also to the kinds of aesthetic approaches most appropriate to a genuinely 'socialised' theatre. Any theatre practitioner who has addressed the obstructiveness and unsuitability of its present administrative and production systems will know that 'art always comes last'. There is a very real sense in which financial, organisational and logistic problems have to be cleared away before the creative work can begin. Instead of the administrative considerations following as a consequence of artistic decisions, there is almost a sense under presently prevailing conditions, in which one has to be politically irresponsible or wilfully blind if one wishes to pursue one's artistic purposes directly. Even this book, having posited the idea of a more socially integrated theatre at its beginning, has had to work through a large number of analytical and practical questions before being able to consider the aesthetic questions which are its ultimate concern. Even then the fullest, most open-minded and objective account of community theatre would, I believe, have to acknowledge that no prescription for a single kind of theatre appropriate to its aims is possible. Prescription of this kind can in any case lead very quickly to proscription.

Indeed, the practice of community theatre companies and the arguments of this book suggest that the term 'community theatre' is not descriptive of a particular kind of product or show, nor implies any particular aesthetic model, but refers rather to the process *behind* the work, to the relationship of a company's work as a whole to its community and to relations of production within the company itself. As suggested earlier, however, these considerations necessarily affect the product in one way or another in any kind of theatre, and community theatre is no exception. Is it possible then to set any aesthetic parameters within which the majority of community theatre falls? Certainly the suggestion that the content of the work be of some direct interest or relevance to the majority of the population in the company's locality is a common feature of policy, as is the desire to present that content in a popular and entertaining form. Shows that deal with broad contemporary issues like housing or unemployment would fall as much into this category as those which deal with specific local campaigns (to stop a motorway or save a hospital for example), or with the operation of a local industry, like British Steel at Stoke, Theatremobile's asbestos show and my own *Motor Show* (about Fords at Dagenham). This kind of show, often portraying facts and figures as well as decades of historical process, may well rely on the techniques of documentary, caricature, cartoon-style depiction, songs, music and cabaret-style patter to indicate the general trends behind the particular incidents.

But while the larger part of community theatre might treat present-day issues in a broader theatrical style than the mainstream tradition, there are notable exceptions, and the interpretation of 'relevance' and 'popularity' in this connection can be as wide and diverse as the difference between a Welfare State pageant through the streets and a realistic rediscovery of mining community history by Pit Prop or DAC in a trade union club. Companies like Covent Garden Community Theatre or Inner City who perform out-of-doors as well as indoors and also service young audiences will tend to develop a broader, more extrovert style of production, as will companies who perform in pubs and clubs or work from a cabaret-style venue, like the Combination at the Albany. The demands of performing different kinds of shows to specific sections of the community like children, tenants or pensioners flatly contradict the idea that there is one singular and distinctive form of community theatre. The nettle to be grasped here is that the needs of the community itself – as in any community taken as a whole – are many and varied.

At the same time, however, the effect of continuity in a company's work – of developing an identity recognisable to one's audience, of centring resources around an administrative and possibly performing base, and of developing a 'mainstream' style both for general audiences and as a distinct alternative to the conventional mainstream – does lead to the suggestion of certain guiding principles, though I suspect that these are as open to personal taste and prejudice as any initiative in theatre inevitably is. For many individual artists the struggle to find and fulfil their own personal artistic vision can lead to the rejection or dismissal of other artists' work. Understandable though that is as part of their own creative process, it is an unsatisfactory basis for objective critical comment. What follows therefore is an account of certain personal aesthetic preoccupations which have been thrown up in the course of fifteen years' experience in and around this field of work.

Inside outside

While the present proliferation of small-cast, one-set dramas about the personal lives of middle-class people is largely irrelevant to the majority of the population, this doesn't mean that they need necessarily be so, nor indeed that large-cast multi-set epics rooted in working-class culture are any more relevant. Quite apart from the question of an audience's actual interest in the surface subject-matter of a play, however, is the point that plays are very rarely in effect about what they seem to be about. I have seen a play ostensibly about the imprisonment of a political activist, the dramatic dynamic of which was ultimately middle-class guilt; I have also seen a play ostensibly about a labour leader's fidelity to his grass roots which was in fact about a theatre company's difficulty in establishing links with the labour movement; I myself have frequently written 'historical' plays for which the motivation has sprung from the desire to tackle contemporary concerns. The reason for people being drawn to a particular 'subject' often proves finally to sing out more from a play than the subject itself. For playwrights or companies devising collectively, there is consequently no greater skill than learning to become conscious of one's real preoccupations. In the question of content then, the present intellectual and emotional disposition of the author or authors is as important as its 'subject'. This is crucial to the business of commissioning plays, and puts the lie to the belief that simply by paying a writer to go away and work for a few weeks, a script satisfactory to either author or company will emerge. Commissioning depends on a close and personal dialogue between author and company, a genuine mutual engagement with each other's concerns, and a lot of time.

A play that treats broad social themes offers no guarantee *in itself* that it will serve a socially broad audience. The experience it's rooted in and the things the playwright passionately cares about are more likely to count in the end. If the writer has direct experience of, say, working-class life and conditions, the chances that what ultimately emerges will speak engagingly to a working-class audience increase considerably. One can see how the converse of this class bias works at present simply by contrasting the difficulty experienced in our predominantly middle-class culture by writers whose strengths lie in reflecting working-class life when they proceed from a once-off success and attempt to develop a consistent body of work without importing a middle-class viewpoint, against the ease and consistency with which this can be achieved by those working within their own culture. To conclude from such an observation however that only working-class writers can write about the working class, that only women can write about women or only black people on black issues, is to deny the very quality of empathy which makes playwriting possible in the first place.

Plays, then, always possess an 'inward' face, however important their 'outward' qualities. It is a curious imbalance in our present theatre practice, however, that where plays – from the reading of scripts through to performance – are most frequently seen and judged by their *ostensible* subject, the whole emphasis of our acting is *inwardly* directed. From acting school and amateur dramatic society to fringe and conventional theatre, the emphasis for actors in instruction and production is on 'digging into' the characters – often irrespective of whether there is, in the writing, any character to dig into. Consequently our assumptions about performance values in British theatre are heavily influenced by the 'reality' of what we see on stage before us. The fact that what we see is fiction (if you see what I mean) is far less openly declared than in European or Oriental theatre, and the truism that many writers inevitably take as their starting-point the observation of life around them *from the outside* is often held against them. Given that the very act of authorship necessarily imposes a personal consistency on a play (whether this is conscious, well-crafted and well-realised or not), it would seem rather more rational to encourage the plays to be inwardly sound and the acting to *dig out* what's in them than to encourage the situation we have at present. Our theatre would be richer – and possibly achieve a greater 'outward' contact with its public if it were thus freed to concentrate on, and were more versed in, the skills of outward presentation. The danger here is that a more expressive theatre can serve merely as a simple release of internal tensions, without tackling the problems of the wider conflicts which produce it. Rather like the pop singer who cries 'I want you, I need you' to an audience who reply 'Yes, yes' in recognition, it's possible for attitudes to be expressed in an immediately satisfactory way but ultimately to reinforce the emotional dependence of their public.

We are nevertheless so used at present to the present 'hothouse' school of production, where audiences are expected to be drawn *into* the world of the play, that it is quite possible for a sane, rational and unphilistine spectator to sit throughout a performance (as Michael Frayn once noted in the *Observer*) just waiting for a door-handle to come off or the scenery to fall down. That actors and audience alike are required to 'hang their wits up in the cloakroom' as Brecht puts it, is a sad reflection on the partial nature of the experience offered in our theatres. The possibility also that a play's characters might have an intellectual life, particularly one quite contrary to their 'actual' situation (a common enough phenomenon in real life) is an element of theatre sadly under-explored in our present-day theatre. Confrontation is invariably between simple, one-note statements of character (however 'well-rounded', however 'deep'), consigning such elements as doubt, hesitancy, contrariness and unpredictability to the catch-all epithet 'inconsistent'.

One of life's most vital and least malleable qualities – its inconsistency – is thus reduced to a boo-word.

Do we have lift-off?

The sixties sense of being 'locked into' a banal, one-plane reflection of reality is clearly still with us, but besides the contradiction, touched on earlier, of a theatre which urges its audience to be critical of a reality it subconsciously enjoys, there is a further dimension – this time in the matter of form – which applies particularly to socialist and working-class theatre. Often in the pursuit of new forms to express socalist or working-class content, companies have recourse to 'popular' forms identified with working-class culture. The problem here is that music-hall, popular music, stand-up comedy, musicals and even thrillers and westerns are all forms which have hardened and set as a result of the way in which capitalist production relations harness popular imagination and talent. Consequently their strongest performance values are those of the 'hard sell', and to achieve these values you end up apeing the very qualities you're trying to get away from. A similar problem exists in assumptions about working-class audiences. Just because our middle-class culture tends to be ultra-sophisticated, depressingly contradictory and subtle to the point of invisibility, this does not mean a culture for the working class should be crude, simplistic and obvious. Indeed, if one of the purposes of socialism is to abolish the conditions of production which necessitate a working class in the first place, why be so enthusiastic about forms which not only perpetuate a separate working-class culture but also speak of obsolete production relations in our own industry? Similar questions dog women's and black culture. While the rediscovery and focus on 'separatist' culture can lead to an increased self-awareness and confidence amongst oppressed groups, that very emphasis on and consciousness of present-day divisions can both exacerbate them and delay the realisation of these groups' aims within the *whole* of society. Once again it is clear that mere critical recognition of imbalances in our culture does not of itself offer a creative solution. The notion that a kind of die-hard emotional commitment to oppression as currently analysed is somehow more militant or revolutionary than successful organisation towards change, is a recipe for increasing ghettoisation. The imaginative and inspirational element, so necessary if one is to see beyond present conditions, is missing.

Dario Fo has touched on a similar question in his talk 'On Popular Theatre' (Milan 1974), dealing there with the element of alertness, of the free and *thinking* spirit of the actor behind the character and its inability to step outside the context of a show and relate directly to the immediate presence of the audience. In that piece Fo deals at length with the question of 'asides' and rightly identifies their demise with the advent of pious respectability in the theatre. Even the radical end of our contemporary theatre is guilty of presenting self-contained, 'consistent' and neatly packaged *pensées*, locked behind a proscenium arch, inside an actors' 'hothouse' or a sophistic ideology at which solemnly 'right-on' audiences nod wisely and see only the emperor's new clothes.

Stripping the emperor

This is not just a question of illusion and anti-illusion, of ironic acting, of Brechtian alienation, of addressing the audience and so on. It is first and foremost a matter of the stage context in which actors and audience inter-relate. In the wrong place at the wrong time, asides can seem fatuous; Brechtian audience address, instead of inviting relaxed thought, can add up to a row of stony-faced automata intimidating their audience. When an actor first walks on stage he has nothing but himself. He is John Smith, actor, a bag of flesh and bones, a real person speaking in front of a group of equally real people. Whatever his costume or disguise, it is that actual presence that the audience reacts to in the first place. Whether he's good-looking, whether he's got a hole in his trousers, whether the door-knob will come away in his hand. Michael Denison and Dulcie Gray used to be applauded before they even opened their mouths. There is a natural delight in being aware of the person under the disguise, just as for schoolchildren it is a delight to discover that teacher is a human being. That excitement is unique to theatre and demands that at some level, depending on the place and material, John Smith acknowledge it because, having got on stage, whatever John Smith does will be seen or overheard. He cannot 'be himself' because the acting area and the lights have prepared the audience for something special. It may appear to be a one-sided conversation, but the very 'presence' of John Smith is dependent on the actual presence of the audience – it is his way of acknowledging them. It is almost a form of politeness; certainly the failure to 'sense' the audience is tantamount to ignoring someone who's expecting you to talk to him. Any suggestion of a theatre form which hopes in some way to 'go out' to its audience, to appeal beyond the confines of the reality it reproduces to the conscious faculties of its audience, has to take this relationship into account. Nothing is more dishonest than an 'outfront' show which is so rigidly fixed and drilled that it makes no difference whether the audience throw bouquets or rotten tomatoes.

For an actor, then, to look at his audience as he would normally at people in the same room with him, to speak from the whole of his person to the whole of theirs, would be to restore the dignity and humanity driven out of theatre by packaging, directorial 'concept', naturalistic 'consistency' in texts and the 'hothouse' school of acting. There is a look of interest, of openness, of relaxed alertness that comes into people's eyes when they are enjoying each others' company. They *want* to know about each other, find out, learn, enrich their own lives, enjoy themselves, just through talking and being in each other's company. The seemingly simple art of conversation is as lacking in today's theatre as anywhere else.

A new aesthetic approach which enabled actors to conduct this kind of 'conversation between equals', to look their audience in the eye even when clowning or when their characters are gripped by anger, fear or insanity, is a potential held by theatre alone. But again the importance of the theatre's production relations re-asserts itself. How can actors held in the thrall of a hierarchical production system, a directorial concept or a naturalistic strait-jacket, look their audience in the eye? How can they or their audiences believe in a liberated, socialist art if it turns the people who make it into mere objects on show? One of my own first experiences in conventional theatre under a supposedly socialist director working on a socialist classic was, when replying to an actor's enquiry about a particular line, to be castigated for 'talking to *his* actors'. Individual contributors' belief in the ideas which the product purports to represent – so crucial to the successful realisation of those ideas on stage – can be destroyed if it is produced in a contradictory fashion. Directors whose productions are liberating but whose methods are oppressive, like feminists who exploit the labour of their female office-staff as badly as any man, impair the credibility of their ostensible aims. In this sense, lasting changes in the arts are more likely to come about through a change in production relations which frees the stance of performers to their material and to their audience than through the simple content of the work.

This primary question of context relates nevertheless not only to production relations and the kind of auditorium and audience one is playing, but also to the overall manner, style and 'voice' of dramatic presentation. In attempting to break out of the 'naturalistic strait-jacket' for example, companies have often used music unthinkingly. In the cause of making shows 'popular', songs have sometimes been considered *de rigueur* and have been grafted on to a basically *prosaic* text with scant consideration for any organic link between the two approaches.* Similarly, within dance- or movement-oriented productions, the use of 'natural' dialogue can seem grossly inappropriate.

Rather like the difficulty of turning improvisation into text described in Chapter Seven, the essential question behind the mixing of dramatic forms is whether their basic approach is 'inward' or 'outward'. Music and dance are often at root about a performer *expressing* a particular state of mind. Against that, the purpose of dialogue as an expression of character, situation and plot is often to explore or *go into* a set of relationships. The jump from one to the other can therefore amount to a very sharp change of dynamic within a performance, unless the context is well considered. Sometimes that jump can be an intentional part of the piece's aesthetic approach – a kind of shock-tactic. On other occasions the transition from 'ordinary dialogue' to a more lyrical mode can be prepared for by increased focus on a character's internal tensions, which then virtually *demand* expression. But the essential clue to the satisfactory mixing of these approaches lies in whether the juxtaposition of different modes is justified by a unifying 'voice' or manner. Brecht's characters can sing because the unfolding of dramatic tension in his plays often depends on a powerful statement of his characters' subjective interests, so that the point arrives where they have to state these directly. In American musicals a sense of extrovert energy informs even the dialogue, so that song comes to represent almost nothing more than the simple addition of musical notes and a formal rhythm. In Bart's *Oliver* and Joan Littlewood's work, the sense of Cockney 'voice' almost made the transition into song a seemingly 'natural' development.

The relation between characters' internal consistency and their outward face is therefore crucial to any kind of theatre which goes out to its audience. On the one hand it is important for the actor that there is a strong core of characterisation which enables the character to stand with its own feet on the ground – a degree of realism which also enables an audience to orient itself within the terms of the piece overall. On the other hand it is important that characters are not consequently so 'land-bound' that they cannot lift out of the mundane, and that audiences – who go in the expectation of something different, something special – are taken away from and beyond the familiar.

In this way the element of imagination, so integral to the pursuit of theatre for both actors and audience, can be fully realised. The exact and literal portrayal of working-class life, so important historically to a naturalist theatre seeking to impress the reality of conditions amongst the poor on an early-twentieth-century, bourgeois audience, can act as a major depressant in the present day to a working-class audience who know those conditions only too well. It is not that exact portrayal which is most important, but the element of imagination which can envisage things differently, appeal to the fantasy and energy of its audience to go beyond present conditions, and

---

*For a fuller account of this problem, see my article, *Brecht and the Broadway Beat* in *Gambit Vol 10, No 38.*

thus act as the truer inspiration. Provided it is rooted in a recognisable and convincing view of reality, its vision can offer a persuasive account of a changed world.

A collective aesthetic

In talking so far about 'the actor' in the singular, I have neglected an aspect of contemporary life which is perhaps more significant in the pursuit of community theatre than any other. While most of our contemporary drama continues to focus on individual 'heroes' or central characters, and many of its situations are one-to-one or one-to-two confrontations, the significant situations which affect most of our lives in reality are not of this kind. Where once kings and princes slugged it out as individuals, farmers ploughed their own patch, craftsmen worked in their own workshops, families were dominated by a single patriarch and business deals were done by two individuals behind closed doors, the reality of our present-day world is very different. Government is by cabinet, land is increasingly owned and worked by companies, manufacture is carried out on the production line, a wife's earnings and child benefit are often significant contributions to the family budget, while most aspects of public life are controlled by decisions taken in committee and carried out in offices. In this context Hamlet's decision-making process seems decidedly anachronistic. Our lives today are much more public and the situations we find ourselves in are, if not always democratic, then at least increasingly collective in the strictly literal sense. The connectedness and inter-dependence between ourselves and others has become more and more significant.

Working-class life has been subject to this tendency longer than that of any other class. Living back-to-back and working in factories and offices, working-class people developed a *modus vivendi* which took for granted that one would be surrounded by relatives, friends, neighbours and workmates every hour of the day. People calling by to borrow food or money, saying hello in the street, looking after each other's children, cracking jokes at work about mutual problems, buying each other drinks in the pub – all of which is a far cry from the lonely careerism of the middle class, often geographically separated from family roots, its private life behind drawn curtains, its children not allowed in the street, and a lonely whisky-bottle for its drinking habit. It was, I believe, Dürrenmatt who observed that tragedy is no longer possible in a society where divorce, abortion, insurance and pension schemes are. It is no accident that the skills of stand-up comedy seem a natural extension of those of the factory joker, the public-bar raconteur, or the 'life' of a family party. The more one lives the realities of economics and power in concert with others, the greater the release offered by wit and humour and the more one develops an 'eye' for character and an 'ear' to the responses of others. At the same time one learns to pitch one's own responses towards the common dialogue and to develop a public 'persona' to mediate between personal concerns and commonly accepted norms.

A more collaborative and socialised context of theatre production offers the prospect of a similar release. If the aim of a show's content in community theatre is to refer in some way to the broad concerns of the majority of the community, many of the old notions of 'dramatic unity' are immediately assaulted. In a highly mobile and fast-changing society, with increased specialisation and high access to information through television, the disparity between situation and aspiration, between opportunity and achievement, between consciousness of events and the power to influence them, grows ever-wider. It is quite possible nowadays to be highly educated, extremely well qualified and chronically unemployed. It is possible to be supremely competent and knowledgeable in a particular job and yet know nothing – or be able to do nothing – about its application in society. The 'community' in its widest sense, is made up of an infinite number of specialist interests and skills growing more and more remote from each other as that community develops and expands in the manner of an exploding star. Instead of dealing with one particular cluster in that complex (as does, say, the bourgeois four-hander psychological drama), theatre which hopes to deal searchingly with the whole of our community has to come to terms with the *connections between* different sections of society. Instead of remaining content with the close-up depiction of an immediate reality, it has to be looking for trends behind that reality. From the agit-prop show for a particular local campaign to the exploration of social change in personal or family life, the emphasis is on *articulating* issues so that the tensions behind them become public, rather than relying on the irresolution or 'mystery' of conflict to create a *dramatic* tension and thus internalise or 'privatise' the issue.

Not only is a broader and more explicit social canvas required, therefore, but the centring of an audience's identification on the personal situation of an individual or small group within society can only approach this quality of social connectedness if what is off-stage is, as it were, present and speaking through what is onstage. In '*Will Wat, if not, what will?*', one of the first shows I wrote for the Half Moon, this approach is summed up in the very curiosity of the title. Wat Tyler is shown fleetingly on stage, but the eventual victors of the Peasants' Uprising of 1381, the rising merchant class, are shown gaining their advantage through a number of different characters and in a wide variety of situations. The peasant class is shown in a similarly anonymous way, and the interest for the audience lies not so much in rediscovering a piece of the East End's history (the original reason for doing the show) through identification with an individual, but through individuals who, variously and from time to time, carry the advance of the interests of the common people on their shoulders. The attempt is to create a dramatic excitement and involvement in the shared fate of a group of people – as with the convict women in *Female Transport* or the pirate crew in the second half of *Women Pirates*. Within this dramatic context the unities of time, place, action and character are secondary to the unity of collective interest. Plays which range over forty to sixty years, move location from country to country and in which characters grow up, die and are replaced by others as in *The Motor Show* or *Passed On* (about the history of the Lollards) attempt to appeal to a core of common interest rather than pin identification on a particular, necessarily fallible individual.

This also has consequences for the structure and form of the plays. If their action is ranging over a wide geographical or historical scope, the unity of their social view may well need to be pulled together through a narrator or some kind of narrative function. The position of narrator – halfway between the play's internal action and its audience – is significant, since it is another way of taking the play *to* the audience. Instead of the audience passing like Alice through the looking-glass from its own world into the world of the play, a midway forum is created to which both worlds simultaneously relate. No longer are an author's private vision and an actor's personal enthusiasm the object of the audience's voyeuristic attention; instead, the publicness of the occasion is acknowledged, and knowledge of particular events and incidents is shared and related to that common forum, 'the floor', as it were, 'of the house'.

All the methods of 'taking out' a show to its audience, so common in community theatre, share this function – be they songs, asides, monologues, narration or direct audience address. And they are all as traditional as theatre itself. The notion that such explicitness in theatre is 'didactic' or a kind of cultural totalitarianism is peculiar to our age and society and probably a product of the continuing fear in 'polite' English society (despite the abolition of the Lord Chamberlain) of the direct, open, democratic and accountable freedom of speech which the medium of theatre – these days almost exclusively – offers. The idea that it is more aesthetically pleasing to articulate social conflict obliquely or surreptitiously – either by clothing it in the complexity of personality or by 'sugaring the pill' – no doubt reflects such grand old English traditions as anti-intellectualism, social hypocrisy, stiff upper lips and rigorous potty training. The masochism of restraint implicit in such 'gentlemanly' attitudes is a luxury which those for whom earning a living is a desperate and urgent affair cannot afford, and is quite different from the aesthetic wisdom of choosing to reflect rather than 'cook' the reality presented, or offering rather than imposing its interpretation. Rather than draw the audience *into* a private vision of the world which creates its own 'reality' (a kind of totalitarianism in itself), the general approach taken by community theatre is to take *out* an interpretation of a broader social reality, often collectively arrived at, the final test of which occurs on 'the floor', that midway zone where the interests of actors and audience are addressed equally.

The consequence of not only a more public subject-matter but also a more public form, allied with the purpose of demonstrating the social connectedness mentioned above, is to suggest a more pluralistic aesthetic. Plays centred on groups of people where their collective fate is important rather than that of an individual character, offer the opportunity for a new kind of dramatic dynamic, more relevant to our contemporary existence. I have tackled this kind of quality in plays of my own like *Landmark* (about the varying responses of a former teenage gang faced, as adults, with the siting of nuclear missiles in their 'own back yard') or *How the Peace was Lost* (about the dissipation of a sense of 'community' amongst Londoners after the Second World War), but there is a similar quality in Wesker's *Kitchen*, David Storey's *The Contractor*, Brecht's *Days of the Commune*, Mustapha Matura's *One Rule* and much of O'Casey's drama. The context of the dramatic dialogue in these plays is one where their 'publicness' is already acknowledged, where the characters speak not so much to each other as individuals (as in the torrid one-to-one simplicity of bourgeois drama) but, as it were, to 'the floor' of their common concerns. It is as if everything said by one character to another can be overheard and shared by anyone and everyone. In an environment where walls are thin, accommodation crowded and people live and work on top of each other, this comes as a natural quality. What each individual says becomes an articulation of part of the common predicament. Values are held in common and so characters come to complement each other collectively, and it is the *sum* of their words and deeds which is most important. At the same time the quality of this kind of dialogue, the act of speaking to 'the floor', of being overheard, because it is an informal kind of public speaking, is not a far cry from turning out and addressing that other public forum, the audience.

Within such a context an actor's work on his role becomes slightly different from conventional acting. While a part may be worked up in isolation to a certain extent, it is the inter-action with others which finally determines how the whole is seen in public. The necessary strong core of characterisation is developed primarily in response to others, involving a greater sensitivity to all the other characters on stage, not just the one being addressed. It also involves a keen sense of what distinguishes the different personal interests and motivations of characters from their public appearance and effect. They are two-way characters, involving a certain lateral thinking. They speak the language of people doing two things at once – the language of people shouting over machine-noise, talking over the garden fence while hanging up washing, feeding the baby while answering the phone, giving directions while laying bricks. Unlike the morbidity of characters on stage doing only one thing, so totally absorbed in their present dilemma that possibilities are strictly limited, a number of possibilities for change are present in the varied skills and ideas of the whole group; the situation is powered by the innate excitement of people as a whole struggling to tackle the collective task in hand.

Most people most of the time, whatever they're doing, have the rest of their lives in the backs of their minds. Rather like guests at a party, they engage in the immediate conversation but are aware of the totality of all the people around them. The ability to remain firm in the 'persona' of the character, yet speak to 'the floor' or turn out to the audience, also gives the opportunity for characters to open up the world of their personal thoughts, for the world of the mind and imagination to be tackled on stage, and thus to transcend the immediate 'reality'. Much of the wit and humour, the caring perceptiveness and the irony of working-class life is based in this two-edged acknowledgement of an immediate situation and the spirited imagination which sees beyond it. The potential for expressing within this kind of form how the world might be different is thus much greater.

It is, however, a more complex form. The successful organisation of five or more equally weighted characters on stage without a given 'pecking order' to explain why some dominate and others respond is a technical challenge – for writers, directors and actors alike. Maintaining a through-line of characterisation when a character's actual lines represent only one fifth or sixth of the text requires a particular kind of skill. If there is to be a key to the potential chaos of everyone chipping in *ad lib*, if art is to make some aesthetically satisfying order of this complex kind of reality, and if the audience is to be able to orient itself within the total picture, characterisation has to involve not just the interpretation of individual lines but an identification with the general mood, atmosphere or idiom presented. For it is this *general* interest which will be the central point of identification for the audience; their interest will be in following the fate of the group as a whole and in relating individual characters to that. Just as people in real life walk into a room and respond (or not!) to the mood prevailing in it, so text and acting in this form of theatre have to take account of the general 'pitch' of a scene. The way characters listen is as important as the way they speak.

Consequently there is far less room in this kind of drama for the fiction of the clear-cut, single-minded, 'well-rounded' character beloved of bourgeois drama, who 'represents' a singular attitude, way of thinking or reacting towards the given situation. The one-to-one confrontation of two opposing, individual 'representatives' is far less likely to become romantically idealised into an heroic struggle because the *context* of that confrontation is ever-present, by which the audience is physically and constantly reminded of its limitations and likely consequences. Characters will never be 'well-rounded' because they will be seen to switch and change according to which other element of the total picture is exerting pressure at the time. Characters, as in reality itself, will be fractured and contradictory, flexible and slippery, and will be seen, as in reality, to respond or not to peer group pressure. They will relate not simply on a personal and emotional level but also consciously. They will duck and weave, bob and manoeuvre, jostle each other, sometimes striking out on their own and sometimes attempting to manipulate each other. The way people 'think' each other before they even begin to relate, for example, could play a part in this dynamic. The upper-middle-class character who *assumes* certain qualities in people with regional accents, the older person who *assumes* a patronising attitude towards a younger one, the lefty who *assumes* an attitude of mind in anyone who contradicts his sacred political tenets can all be seen in their presumption because the collective social context of these encounters, the 'reality' they are in fact addressing will be articulated.

Speaking with one voice

The form that articulation takes is also crucial. The question of treating theatre as an open, accessible and candid form also has consequences for the nature of dialogue. The more one sees dramatic performance not as a thing apart but as part of a public dialogue, the less relevant become traditional literary qualities in the written text. Commentators on theatre frequently denigrate the play which is 'no more than a political pamphlet' but are far less sharp-witted in identifying the play which is essentially a novel, an internal monologue or an epic poem in dialogue form. Much of the rebellion amongst young actors in the early seventies against the 'Writer' was against a form of writing which used the actor as a literary mouthpiece rather than offered a reality which actors themselves could take hold of and use. The reality in theatre which everyone present relates to is actual performance – where the pudding is eaten and proven. Dialogue which offers a clear portrayal of character and situation for actors to use and for the audience to identify, but also allows for fluidity and spontaneity in performance, is the dialogue which makes greatest use of the particular advantages of theatre and which holds the greatest potential for vivacity and a sense of danger in production. This is not to say there is no place for fine writing in itself, but its best place is where it extends and heightens an already firmly rooted stage reality.

This quality is for me best demonstrated by reference to translation and adaptation. In my own work I discovered early on that many existing translations of Brecht's plays by scholars and academics simply did not capture the life and theatrical vigour of Brecht's dialogue. Either too literary or too remote, their language belied the 'popular' element of the play's content. Similarly, when translating a play like Harald Mueller's *Big Wolf* (written in a theatrical amalgam of German working-class argots), I was conscious of a process not of simple transliteration from one language into another, but of transposing the *effect* of Mueller's dialogue within bourgeois German theatre into our own tradition. My task in adapting Lope de Vega's *Fuente Ovejuna* for the Tom Allen Centre was to retain the import of the original story (about the overthrow of a tyrannical lord by a village community), but at the same time to couch it in behaviour and language which were vivid for a contemporary East End audience. *Back Street Romeo* for the Half Moon went even further, taking only the structure of Shakespeare's story and transforming it into a parable about two conflicting traditions in East End culture – the cab-driver/gangster tradition and the trade unionist/socialist one.

In each of these adaptations it was crucial to find the 'voice' which spoke for both characters in the plays and for the audience. In plays where the central interest of the action lies with a collection or group of people, the unifying effect of language becomes even more important. Since the dominant 'voice' or idiom of the play, through which the audience connects with it, will be predominantly that of the social group amongst whom the play is set, the dialogue of each individual character will necessarily assume its own relation to this central 'pitch' or norm. For the majority of characters, the group amongst whom the play is predominantly set, this will mean a form of language which is held in common and shared, where individual characters effectively complement each other's contribution to the meaning of the play as a whole. Instead of the onus of meaning in the play being in the literary and idealised language of single-minded, individual 'representatives' of particular and typical attitudes, the dialogue can proceed more realistically through a series of partial, perhaps broken, certainly more colloquial utterances, of which the *sum* is both the voice of that group and the unity of form through which the audience connects with the play. This will involve a responsiveness and sensitivity to the way people in real life complement and contradict each other's meanings in their conversation and behaviour towards each other – a sensitivity to the inflections of everyday speech, the way suggestion is conveyed through nuance, tone of voice, gesture and physical stance, and is either picked up and confirmed or rejected by others. It involves a keen eye and ear for what separates the various personal interests and motivations of characters from their public effect, as well as for the way their common social context in turn affects their interests and aspirations. It means not only attention to people's roots and backgrounds in a static sense but also to how they develop and change in inter-action with each other. It is a form of stage realism where not just material circumstances but the actual physical presence of other people modifies the characters' behaviour. If the 'reality' before the audience's eyes is not to be 'cooked', this stage reality has to possess a certain autonomy. The evidence of the characters' behaviour and speech in front of both the actors' and the audiences' eyes is the common factor to which both can relate equally. It acknowledges the way in which people's actions and attitudes are shaped in reality but also plays to the strengths of live theatre. In this way it can sensitise its audience in a very palpable way to the ways in which we construct our lives through the sum of our social responses to each other, a sum which is ultimately not just our immediate surroundings but society as a whole.

Since the norm through which this happens is a social construct rather than simply an authorial view of reality, its language will need to be accessible on as broad a social plane as possible. It needs to be able to 'open out' to its audience and be approachable by them. It needs to strike chords of recognition in its audience, who may then – through points of sympathy and involvement with individual characters – be led to consideration of the situation as a whole. It is interesting in this respect to consider a distinctive feature of the difference between working-class and middle-class speech. Living and working in close proximity with others and having to respond directly to immediate pressures with little time to reflect and little opportunity of altering their circumstances, working-class communities tend to fall into a style of speech which is primarily reactive. It is in the first instance like a cry of pain, a complaint or a 'moan' about what's being done to them rather than any attempt – as is more usual amongst people who can influence their circumstances – to affect, change or manipulate their given situation. A remark like 'Bloody hot in here, innit' for example, would be a direct response to the temperature of a room and does not, of itself, anticipate a personalised response. It is lobbed, as it were, to 'the floor', where others may respond or not as they wish. The frequent use of 'isn't it', 'don't I', 'aren't we' etc. in working-class speech is a reflection of the need to consult and confirm with others before something (like opening the window!) gets done. While its manner of expression is very blunt and direct, it doesn't *assume* a positive response. If indeed no response is forthcoming from 'the floor', this may imply the issue isn't important enough for others to waste their breath on.

It is an approach which addresses the objective situation directly, leaving space for a collective response, similar to the Marxist distinction between bourgeois democracy and working-class democracy, in that the former implies equal rights for individuals regardless of each individual's personal wealth and power, while the latter implies the subordination of individual will to the needs of the class as a whole. For actors it suggests a firmly anchored characterisation influencing and being influenced through this common language by both other characters and audience. For the audience it implies an invitation to become part of 'the floor', to engage and connect through a common idiom with the collective fate of the characters.

The sense of an open forum then, within which the voice that simply experiences or responds to the common situation is as important as the voice which thinks it knows, or attempts to do, something about it – that for me is the most exciting, and radically alternative, aesthetic approach which the different production relations of community theatre offer from conventional theatre. The dramatic possibilities of the 'free zone' of the imagination become truly opened up when *any* response to the world we live in, whether bluntly emotional or systematically rational, is not only permissible in theory but actually demonstrable in practice. The chances of a theatre which can address the whole of the community on matters which concern the whole of the community then become that much greater, as does the possibility of theatre finding a new and vital function within our increasingly compartmentalised and insulated society. /